CONNIE CLARK

50 prayer services

for middle schoolers

for every season of the Church year
and more

TWENTY THIRD 23rd
PUBLICATIONS
NEW LONDON, CT 06320
WWW.23RDPUBLICATIONS.COM

TWENTY-THIRD PUBLICATIONS
A Division of Bayard
One Montauk Avenue, Suite 200
PO Box 6015
New London, CT 06320
(860) 437-3012 or (800) 321-0411
www.23rdpublications.com

ISBN 978-1-58595-876-4

All music suggestions are from Oregon Catholic Press (OCP), 5536 NE Hassalo, Portland, OR 97213-3638. For more information, visit www.ocp.org.

Library of Congress Cataloging-in-Publication Data

Clark, Connie, 1961-
  50 prayer services for middle schoolers : for every season of the Church year and more / Connie Clark.
     p. cm.
  ISBN 978-1-58595-876-4
  1. Middle school students—Prayers and devotions. 2. Church year—Prayers and devotions. 3. Catholic Church—Prayers and devotions. 4. Prayer—Catholic Church. I. Title. II. Title: Fifty prayer services for middle schoolers.
  BV283.S3C43 2012
  242'.63—dc23
              2012026201

Printed in the U.S.A.

CONTENTS

Life in the middle ages

Have you ever wondered why there's only one story in the Bible about Jesus during his adolescence? My husband thinks it's because even God doesn't want to talk about those tumultuous teenage years.

Middle schoolers are poised at the brink of those years. And those of us who teach, parent, or otherwise lead them in faith have days when we'd rather not talk about them either.

You often hear the teen years described as something like the morning of life. If that's true, then the middle school years are the alarm clock that wakes us up a half an hour too early.

We just never seem ready for sixth-grade girls who are suddenly wearing mascara, or eighth-grade boys who could use a shave. And they're just as surprised and befuddled by all these crazy new emotions, growth spurts, and complexities of life as the rest of us.

Even our story about the twelve-year-old Jesus in the temple is full of contradictions, not just for his unsuspecting parents, but also for all those people in the temple who are wowed by his knowledge of Scripture.

Like the people in the temple, we in religious education need to adjust our thinking when it comes to middle schoolers. Study after study of "tweens" and their religious practices shows that their attitudes toward faith, prayer, religion, and God are changing radically—just as their bodies, minds, emotions, environment, technology, and everything else is in flux. If you've spent any time with middle schoolers, you know exactly what I'm talking about.

In short, the middle school years are a tender time. We don't do sixth graders any favors when we drone on and on in prayer. But we can get right to their hearts and souls when we remind ourselves that their attention spans are about five minutes long. Most of our seventh graders tune us out when we talk church history or doctrine, but they'll perk up when we show them that Jesus loves them *today*.

So let me be direct. The prayer services in this book are written for middle schoolers. They're not written for you, or me, or your DRE, or your pastor, or even your principal, as wonderful as all of you are. These prayers are written to break through to kids in sixth, seventh, and eighth grade to help them get to know God, themselves, and all the crazy things going on in their adolescent lives.

The prayers are written in conversational language so students can see that it's OK to speak to God just as they are. You'll also find references kids are familiar with, so if you don't approve of kids using cell phones in class, or you're uncomfortable using words like "yeah" and "really?" in your prayers, you might want to look at some other prayer books. Yeah. Really.

Remember, your goal is to keep middle schoolers loving Jesus and coming back to church. So you'll find your role as an adult leader or teacher in these prayer services lessens as the year goes on. And that's exactly how it should be, as your maturing students take greater ownership of their prayer life.

A meaningful prayer service...

...has a visual focal point, whether it's the church tabernacle, the crucifix in your prayer corner, or a picture in students' minds to meditate on.

...has a calm leader with a steady voice who doesn't move around the room too much (unless you're leading a procession).

...honors everyone's level of participation and respects that a "quiet" student may be experiencing God in ways we can't begin to fathom.

Using these prayers

The prayers in this book are written to be used in parish faith formation programs, Catholic schools, youth groups, and homeschool groups. You can hold these services anywhere—a classroom prayer corner, a church, a hall, a multipurpose room, or a living room.

Most of the services require very little preparation. A few, like the Our Lady of Guadalupe celebration or the Wailing Wall project, might need some planning and supplies. But everything is laid out for you, including any reproducible prayers or scripts to distribute to your students.

Be your own guide

All of the student-speaking parts here are broken into quick dialogue bites. Some can be read by individuals or small groups; others are meant to be read by an entire class. Feel free to adjust these directions to your group, especially directions like "left side" and "right side." Maybe break these parts into "girls" and "guys," or "anyone wearing black" and "anyone wearing pink." In fact, it's a good idea to change things around often, and go "off script," just to keep everyone on their prayer toes.

A few other things you'll need

Of course, you don't need anything to pray other than an open heart. But some things can make group prayer easier:

A Bible or lectionary. If we want kids to read the Bible, we'd better read it ourselves. That's why you won't see the full Scripture readings reprinted here. Whenever a Scripture passage is cited— and there's one in almost every prayer in this book—take the opportunity to be a role model, and read the passage directly from the Bible.

A prayer center or prayer corner. Almost every prayer in this book refers to a class prayer center or corner. Whether your group meets in a classroom, a church hall, a private living room, or even an office, you need a focal point that's easily identifiable as the place to gather for prayer or meditation. It can be a table, a corner, a desk, or a combination of all those things. In many cases, it will have to be taken down from week to week. (It's a good idea to store the elements of your prayer corner in a clear plastic storage container.) And check page 10 for a prayer service that allows students to take ownership of your classroom prayer center. See the Appendix for a guide to setting up your prayer corner.

A Catholic playlist or CD collection. It's not easy to coax middle schoolers into singing, but music is an essential component of group prayer. Try exposing students to contemporary Catholic artists and composers, like Matt Maher, Steve Angrisano, and Sarah Hart, to name just a few. But don't overlook traditional hymns, and even Latin chant. Sure, your kids may roll their eyes at the "church music," but it's a part of our faith, and there are times when it works.

Meditation: Your students need it, and so do you

Sure, their attention spans are about as long as the average Twitter update, but let's not sell middle schoolers short. They can, and will, rise to certain challenges. That's why you'll find so many guided meditations in this book.

Modern human beings need regular, deep meditation to counteract all the multitasking we do. The problem is, no one wants to teach it to a group of raucous, attitudinal tweens and teens. But if we don't teach them this important prayer skill, who else will? And really, it's not hard to do, as long as you speak their language. Here are some things to remember:

- Stay positive. Frame any meditation as "me time" with God. Focus on how this time is all about them and their relationship with God.
- Minimize distractions. Gather anywhere other than their usual seating—which they might associate with learning and hard work, not spiritual contemplation. (Not to nag about it, but a prayer center can be a good place to gather. Just saying.)
- Create plenty of space between students.
- To help them imagine things more clearly, help them picture what's happening as if it were a scene from a movie.
- Practice speaking slowly, calmly, and softly.
- For more information, see "Praying lectio divina with your students" in the Appendix (page 130).

With you at every step

As I wrote this book, I thought of the middle schoolers I've taught over the years and of the kids who will pray these services. And of course, I prayed for you as you lead your students. I really did. I know that Jesus has a special place in his heart for you, as he recalls his days among the teachers of the temple. And I know every time you gather your students in his name, he's there by your side, guiding you, blessing you, and filling you with his peace.

PART 1

Seasonal prayers

STARTING THE SCHOOL YEAR • FALL FEASTS AND REMEMBRANCES
ADVENT AND DECEMBER • CHRISTMAS AND WINTER
LENT • HOLY WEEK • EASTER AND PENTECOST

Beginning candlelight blessing

WHAT YOU'LL NEED

- **candle** *(large enough for students to hold easily)*
- **Bible** *(open to John 1:1–5)*

Controlled chaos. That's the first day of school or religious education classes. So get your students' attention with something different: darkness. Then bring everyone into the calming presence of God with a candlelight prayer service. You'll have a lot to do today, so keep things simple.

Beginning candlelight blessing

After your class has gathered and you've made some introductions, turn down the lights a little. (You'll be reading by candlelight, so don't make it so dark that you can't see at all.) Invite students to stand in a circle around you. Wait for quiet before you begin.

Leader   In the name of the Father, and of the Son, and of the Holy Spirit.

All   Amen.

Leader   Lord, thank you for bringing these wonderful young people here today. I know some of them aren't *quite* as thankful as I am to be here, so I ask you to help them—and all of us—this year. All good things come from you. So we pray for your gifts of wisdom and love. May they lead us back to you in a circle like the one we're forming here.

As we begin our year, let's listen to what God says about beginnings.

(Read John 1:1–5. After the reading, invite everyone to sit and get comfortable wherever they are in the prayer circle.)

Leader   And now, we'll pray.

This is a "beginning" for us, Lord. And we thank you for it. We ask you to bless all of us here. Help us shine in the darkness. We'll pass around this candle as a symbol of our commitment to living in your light this year.

When the candle comes to you, please say your name and what, or who, you'd like to pray for this year. Then we'll all respond, "Send us your light, Jesus."

I'll begin. My name is _____ and I'd like to pray for...

All   Send us your light, Jesus.

(Offer the candle to the person next to you. After the candle returns to you, conclude with the following.)

Leader   Lord Jesus, light of the world, enlighten our minds with your wisdom this year. Help us bring your love to all those we meet. In the name of the Father, and of the Son, and of the Holy Spirit.

All   Amen.

"Chill" with Mom

WHAT YOU'LL NEED

- **Marian statue** *or image*
- **flowers**
- **small plastic pool** *or plastic tubs filled with water*
- **sunscreen**
- **towels** *(optional)*

THINGS TO DO BEFORE CLASS

Create a grotto reminiscent of the famous sanctuary at Lourdes by bringing a statue or image of Our Lady outside and decorating it with flowers. Fill a small inflatable pool or some plastic tubs with water, and let everyone soak their bare feet as you pray. Keep it short, and when you're finished, feel free to splash all you want.

Who says you can't pray while dangling your feet in a pool of cool, clear water? If your class is in session during a heat wave, there's no better way to refresh overheated bodies and parched souls than a retreat with Jesus and his mother. Late summer, after all, is Mary's season, beginning with the feast of her Assumption on August 15, through the feast of her nativity on September 8, to the Memorial of Our Lady of Sorrows on September 15.

But don't limit this prayer service to August. Use it any time temperatures soar and your class needs a quick break from the heat.

"Chill" with Mom prayer service

Gather around the pool of water and let everyone step inside, or have everyone sit back around the side and dangle their feet in the water.

All   In the name of the Father, and of the Son, and of the Holy Spirit. Amen.

Leader   Lord Jesus, we're thanking you for this small relief from the heat. We're remembering that you always take care of us. Just like Mary took care of you. Today, we're thinking about those times when Mary took care of things, whether they were big or small. Our response today is, "Mary took care of it."
     So let's begin.
     When God was looking for someone to be your mother...

All   Mary took care of it.

Leader   When Elizabeth needed help because she was old and having a baby...

All   Mary took care of it.

Leader   Jesus, when you and your friends were at a wedding and the bride and groom ran out of wine...

All   Mary took care of it.

Leader   And Jesus, when you carried your cross and you looked for someone to comfort you in the crowd of screaming, jeering people...

All   Mary took care of it

Leader   When the world needed healing and you needed someone to spread your Gospel in Lourdes, France...

All   Mary took care of it.

Leader   Mary, as we enjoy this little water break, we ask you to take care of those who can't get clean water today. Watch over everyone who suffers in this heat: the elderly, the poor, and those who labor in the hot sun. Give your care to the animals that don't get enough water, and the plants and crops that wilt in the heat.
     We ask you this with our prayer...

All   Hail Mary, full of grace...

Leader   In the name of the Father, and of the Son, and of the Holy Spirit.

All   Amen.

Designing our own place for God

THINGS TO DO AHEAD OF TIME

■ *Print out the prayer service so everyone can follow along.*

■ *Explain that students will create their own prayer space. It will be a place where your group gathers throughout the year to reflect and pray.*

Many teachers create classroom prayer centers from their personal collections of religious items. (See Appendix [page 130] for more information about prayer centers.) So why not give your students a hand in their creation too?

In this two-part service, students ask the Holy Spirit for inspiration, and then they celebrate in prayer. The services themselves are simple. The real work is in the planning. The rewards? Your students are deeply involved and personally invested in your classroom prayer space. Does group prayer get any better than that?

Designing our own place for God (PART ONE)

All   In the name of the Father, and of the Son, and of the Holy Spirit. Amen.
Hey, God, we're trying to find your presence in our lives. We want to make a space here for that. So, Father, can you help us, here?

(Pause for silent reflection.)

All   Holy Spirit, can you inspire us to think of ways to make this prayer center our own?

(Pause for silent reflection.)

All   Jesus, once we've made this prayer center, can you meet us here, and be with us, just as we are?

(Pause for silent reflection.)

All   Thanks. In the name of the Father, and of the Son, and of the Holy Spirit. Amen.

(Now that you've prayed about it, take some time to think about what you can do to make the prayer center a place where you and others can really experience God together. You may want to bring items from home, or create something in class together. Your teacher may also have some ideas. Whatever it is, decide on it together. Remember, the Holy Spirit is inspiring you.)

Designing our own place for God (PART TWO)

All   In the name of the Father, and of the Son, and of the Holy Spirit. Amen.
OK, Lord, we've prayed, we've thought, we've talked. And now we've created this holy place.

(Add items to the prayer center.)

All   So, Lord, it's time for you to do your part, too. Open our hearts to your presence. Open our minds to you. And just be here with us. Thanks. In the name of the Father, and of the Son, and of the Holy Spirit. Amen.

(Take a few moments to sit quietly in your prayer space.)

Can anything good come from this?

WHAT YOU'LL NEED

■ **Bible** *or lectionary*
(open to John 1:45–51)

THINGS TO DO
AHEAD OF TIME

■ *Decide your approach: group discussion or journaling.*

■ *Choose reader volunteers.*

■ *Print out and copy the prayer service script and distribute to your class.*

B ecause this prayer service invites students to discuss potentially sensitive situations, you may choose to break into small groups. Or it may be more useful for students to enter their thoughts in journals.

Can anything good come from this?

Reader 1   (*Read John 1:45–51*)

All   Can anything good come from Nazareth?

Reader 2   Lord, that's what this guy, Nathaniel, said. He had no idea who you were, but he heard "Nazareth" and he started thinking negative thoughts. People do that to us too sometimes, Lord. Just because we're from a certain place, or we dress a certain way, or we have a certain last name, or we're in certain classes, or we're friends with certain people, they think that they know us. But they don't know us at all.

Leader   Has it ever happened to you? Has someone thought they knew you, or made an assumption about you based on something that wasn't very important? Maybe it was based on where you live, what clothes you wear, or who you hang out with. Think about a time when something like that happened to you. If you want, talk about it in your group or write about it in a journal. When you're ready, gather in your group and finish the prayer together.

Reader 3   Lord, this guy Nathaniel was ready to think the worst of you, just because of where you were from. But the town you came from isn't important. What's important is who you are: Jesus, the Son of God.

All   Can anything good come from Nazareth?

Reader 4   Lord, you told Nathaniel you saw him under the fig tree. That totally blew Nathaniel's mind, because he thought he'd been all alone. But you showed him that you—a guy from Nazareth—knew him better than anyone else.

All   Can anything good come from Nazareth?

Reader 5   Jesus, you know all of us better than anyone else does. You know the "real" us. And each one of us is important to you, no matter where we're from or what we've done. Help us stay strong in your love, even when other people misjudge us. And help us look at others the same way you do—with love, respect, kindness, and peace.

All   Can anything good come from Nazareth? Yes, Lord, we believe it does. And we believe we will see the greater things that you promise, in each person we meet. In the name of the Father, and of the Son, and of the Holy Spirit. Amen.

Hello, I'm praying for you today

You can use this prayer at the beginning of the year, or at a midpoint, especially if you notice cliques or students who remain "outsiders."

WHAT YOU'LL NEED

■ **sticker-type nametags**
(if you can, find those that say "Hello, my name is _____")
■ **markers** or pens
■ **blank sheets of paper**

THINGS TO DO AHEAD OF TIME

■ *On your attendance roster, randomly match everyone with a partner. Try to match up students who don't know each other well.*

■ *At the beginning of class, have everyone write their names on the nametags and wear them. Once everyone is seated, call out the name pairs and have everyone meet with their partner. Have each partner switch nametags. They will wear the nametags for the rest of the class. Send everyone back to their partner's seat, so that everyone is now sitting in a different seat. Distribute sheets of paper to all. They can wear the nametags throughout class, but once they take off the nametag, they should affix it to the paper. Make sure each student brings his or her partner's nametag home. Remind everyone to pray for their partners in the evening and before they go to bed.*

■ *You can extend this prayer if you want, by asking the partners to talk with each other, either during this session or the next. If they're comfortable, they can share an intention they'd like their partner to pray for.*

■ *Print out and copy the prayer service script and distribute to your class.*

■ *After everyone has switched nametags and seats, begin your prayer.*

Hello, I'm praying for you today

Leader   In the name of the Father, and of the Son, and of the Holy Spirit.

All   Amen.

Leader   Lord Jesus, thanks for bringing these prayer partners together in your name.

All   Lord Jesus, we're wearing other people's names. We're sitting in other people's places, which feels kind of weird. Help us understand what it's like to walk in someone else's shoes and see the world from someone else's point of view.

(Pause for a moment to think about this.)

All   Lord, we've been paired up with other people today. We may not know our prayer partners very well, but one thing we do know. They have something they need us to pray for. So that's what we're doing, Lord.

(Picture your prayer partner and pray the following in silence for them.)

All   Jesus, I ask you to help my friend today. Give (name of the person you're praying for) courage, strength, and peace. Give (name) good friends, a happy family life, and confidence to do all you ask. Remember (name's) special intentions. Amen.

(Bring your prayer partner's nametag home with you, and continue praying for him or her through the afternoon and evening.)

I am (much more than) a rock

PRAYER FOR OUR CHURCH FAMILY

Your students probably won't get the reference from the old Simon and Garfunkel tune, but they'll enjoy playing with the stones. From this one prayer service you can develop many lessons throughout your year. Create "rock journals," for instance, and let students write about God's call and their response.

WHAT YOU'LL NEED

▪ **several small, flat stones** (you can find them at craft stores or home supply/hardware stores)

▪ **permanent markers** or ink pens

THINGS TO DO AHEAD OF TIME

▪ *Using the marker or pen, write one word or phrase from the list below on each of the stones. (You can add more words if you want.)*

LEARN » **PRAY** » **ACT** » **CHOOSE LIFE** » **SILENCE FORGIVE** » **BE MERCIFUL**

▪ *On your board, write the words or phrases, plus a practical application or promise about them, for example:*

LEARN...*I will keep learning about Jesus and my faith.*

PRAY...*I will pray every day for _____.*

ACT...*I will do something kind for someone every day.*

CHOOSE LIFE...*I will appreciate and protect all life.*

SILENCE...*I will not gossip.*

FORGIVE...*I will forgive.*

BE MERCIFUL...*I will give to the poor and be kind to the weak.*

I am (much more than) a rock

PRAYER FOR OUR CHURCH FAMILY

As you gather, sing or play a recording of a song such as "Be the Hands, the Heart of God," by Mark Friedman and Janet Vogt.

Leader In the name of the Father, and of the Son, and of the Holy Spirit.

All Amen.

Leader Our Catholic Church is Christ's family here on earth. You and I are part of that family. We build our church with one brick or one stone at a time. We build our family with one act of love and one act of faith at a time.

(Distribute the stones. Explain that each one is like a personal call from Jesus. It may not be the stone they wanted or asked for, but sometimes Jesus has something in mind for us that we don't quite understand. Invite students to sit for a few moments in silence and think about what they've been asked to do. When they're ready, each can come forward, one at a time, and place his or her stone in the prayer corner. Over the course of the school year, check in with students and talk about how they are living their call.)

Leader Lord Jesus, help us discover how we fit into your great building project, the Church. Keep us strong so that we can live the life you have planned for us and do the things you ask. In the name of the Father, and of the Son, and of the Holy Spirit. Amen.

Peace begins with me

Make sure you make just one copy of this prayer service so that students actually have to take action and pass it on to the next person in the prayer circle. Each student will have to show the next person where they left off reading the prayer, so that the next person can continue.

Afterwards, ask students why they think you made only one copy of the prayer. Was it because you ran out of printer ink? Or was there another reason?

WHAT YOU'LL NEED

▩ **Bible** or lectionary
(open to John 15:12)

THINGS TO DO AHEAD OF TIME

▩ Print only one copy of the prayer service, and have everyone pass it around as they read it.

OPTIONAL: FOLLOW UP

Create a large cross shape on a poster board or bulletin board. Create a caption that says, "Jesus is the way to true peace." Distribute smaller crosses (cut them out of construction paper, or use foam stickers) to students.

After you've said the prayer together, give each student three crosses. Have them write something they can do to "live peace" on each cross. Examples:

I won't fight with someone in my family for one day.

I'll say "hi" to someone at school that no one talks to.

I'll forgive a friend who hurt me.

Remind them that if they can't think of something, they can pray to Jesus for help. Then have everyone place the crosses on the bulletin board cross. Show how each cross is small, but that they form something really big that can change the world.

Peace begins with me

After you've gathered in your prayer circle, each person reads a section of this prayer and then passes it on to the next person. The only exception is the person who reads the Bible passage. (You might want to keep a Bible close.) As you read or listen to the words, reflect prayerfully on what Jesus is asking you to do.

All   In the name of the Father, and of the Son, and of the Holy Spirit. Amen.

Reader 1   It can begin with one person.
I say something I don't mean.
You throw it back in my face.
Before you know it, we're fighting.

Reader 2   It can begin with one thing.
I want something of yours.
It's not fair that you own this thing and I don't.
I start to think you don't deserve this thing.
So I take it from you.
Before you know it, we're fighting.

Reader 3   It can all begin with one idea.
My idea is right.
I don't understand your idea, and anyway, mine is better.
Before you know it, we're arguing and fighting.

Reader 4   It's so dumb, but it's true.
Wars can start with one person, one thing, or one idea.
Crazy, but true.

Reader 5   But it doesn't have to be this way.

Reader 6   *(Read John 15:12 from the Bible)*

Reader 7   It can begin with one person.
I say something I don't mean. You say something back.
Then I say, "I'm sorry. I didn't mean it. Please forgive me."
And you forgive me.
Before you know it, we're friends again.
And nobody's fighting.

Reader 8 It can begin with one thing.
I want something of yours.
But you're my friend, so I'm happy for you that you own this thing.
Then I look at all I have already.
I think about sharing my own stuff.
Before you know it, you're doing the same thing.
Everybody's sharing. Everybody's happier.

Reader 9 It can begin with one idea.
"Love one another."
Before you know it, there's no more hunger, no more homelessness,
    no more poverty.
Before you know it, we're all living in peace.
All because of one person doing one small thing.

Reader 10 It may sound crazy, but one person can change the world.
One person died for our sins.
One person beat sin and death forever.
One person changed the world, changed eternity.
Jesus is that person.

All God, each of us is just one person. But with you, anything is possible.
With you, one person can be a peacemaker.
That one person is me. Right now.

Right Side But I need your help. So, Jesus, help me love my enemies.
Help me forgive.

Left Side Help me put others first.
Help me remember that we're all the same, even though we may seem
different.

All Help me. I'm one person.
But with you, and with my friends here, I can change the world.
In the name of the Father, and of the Son, and of the Holy Spirit. Amen.

Signs of the cross

EXALTATION OF THE HOLY CROSS, SEPTEMBER 14

This feast commemorates the finding of the Holy Cross by St. Helena, mother of the Roman emperor Constantine. The middle school history curriculum includes Constantine and the rise of Christianity, so you're in good company on this feast day.

WHAT YOU'LL NEED

■ **photograph or image** of the World Trade Center cross, also known as the Ground Zero cross

■ **Bible** or lectionary (open to Philippians 2:5-11)

THINGS TO DO AHEAD OF TIME

■ *Display the image of the Ground Zero cross, and talk about how it was formed out of two crossbeams. For more information, check Wikipedia or google "Ground Zero Cross."*

■ *Plan a walking tour of your school or church grounds, and have students look for intentional or unintentional images of the cross in unlikely places—in tree branches that crisscross, for example, or in window panes that form a cross. Have students work in teams (supervised by an adult) to use their cell phones to take pictures of the crosses they find. Explain that they might have to look at things with a different perspective to spot the crosses.*

■ *When all the teams meet back up, invite students to share their photos.*

Signs of the cross

Gather in church before the main crucifix, around the image of the Ground Zero cross or around your classroom crucifix.

Leader   Lord, we make the Sign of the Cross before we pray, to help us focus on you.

All   In the name of the Father, and of the Son, and of the Holy Spirit. Amen.

Leader   More than 2,000 years ago a wooden cross was slammed into the ground. That cross stopped the power of sin and death forever. Today, Jesus on the cross is as strong as ever. As we pray today, we respond with an old but powerful prayer. Here it is: We adore you, O Christ, and we praise you, because by your Holy Cross you have redeemed the world. Let's repeat it:

All   We adore you, O Christ, and we praise you, because by your Holy Cross you have redeemed the world.

Leader   And now, let's listen to the word of God.

Reader 1   *(Read Philippians 2:5–11)*

Reader 2   Jesus, the sign of your cross is everywhere. We've found it today in places we didn't expect. Help us see that your incredible love follows us wherever we go.

All   We adore you, O Christ, and we praise you, because by your Holy Cross you have redeemed the world.

Reader 3   Jesus, the sign of your cross is everywhere, even in the rubble of the World Trade Center. Help people see that wherever there's sadness and pain, you bring comfort and peace. Even in the most horrible darkness, you will always guide us. Even in death, you give us a new life.

All   We adore you, O Christ, and we praise you, because by your Holy Cross you have redeemed the world.

Reader 4   Jesus, the sign of your cross is everywhere. When we're in trouble or scared, or when we're tempted or we feel weak, help us remember that making the sign of your cross is a way of asking for your strength and protection.

All   We adore you, O Christ, and we praise you, because by your Holy Cross you have redeemed the world.

Reader 5   Jesus, the sign of your cross is everywhere. Inspire us to look at it every day so we can see the incredible love that's there: in your hands, your feet, and your side.

All   We adore you, O Christ, and we praise you, because by your Holy Cross you have redeemed the world.

(Invite students to kneel and gaze at the cross for a few minutes, reflecting on the love that's there and what it means to them. Conclude with the Sign of the Cross.)

Not your grandmother's angels

A LECTIO DIVINA EXERCISE
FEAST OF THE ARCHANGELS, SEPTEMBER 29

WHAT YOU'LL NEED

■ **Bible** *(open to one of the following readings)*

THE ARCHANGEL RAPHAEL
Tobit 12:1–6, 11–22

THE ARCHANGEL GABRIEL
Luke 1:5–22

THE ANGEL OF THE LORD
Luke 2:8–14, Matthew 28:1–8, or Acts 1:9–11

GUARDIAN ANGELS
Psalm 91:9–12

THINGS TO DO AHEAD OF TIME

■ *Read "Praying lectio divina with your students" (see Appendix, page 130)*

Angels have been given all sorts of new identities in our modern world, from delicate Christmas tree decorations to New Age-y, goddess-like beings. Help middle schoolers sort through these images and mature in their understanding of God's glorious messengers, by inviting them to meditate on the Scripture passages that form the Church's teaching on angels and archangels. This prayer service uses the practice of lectio divina (divine reading) to help students meditate on Scripture. For more information on why meditation is so important for middle schoolers, see "Praying lectio divina with your students" in the Appendix.

23

Not your grandmother's angels

Give everyone a few moments to get comfortable. Students can lie on the floor if they want.

Leader We're going to have some "me time" with God. This is all about you and God. So let's begin. In the name of the Father, and of the Son, and of the Holy Spirit. Close your eyes and take a deep breath, in and out. Let everything go from your day. Put aside the things you're worried about. School. Homework. Chores. Problems. This is time for you and God to be alone together. So bring yourself into God's peaceful, loving presence now. Ask the Holy Spirit to be with you and guide you.

(Take a few moments to let everyone be aware of God's presence.)

Leader As I read the following passage from the Bible, I'd like you to listen for any words or phrases that stand out to you.

(Read the passage slowly, gently, and calmly. If you are in a church and students are spread out, use a microphone so you don't have to shout.)

Leader Now I'm going to read this passage again. Listen for those words or phrases, and this time think about what God might be saying to you.

(Read the passage again, slowly, gently, and calmly.)

Leader Think about what you'd like to say to God. Have a conversation with God, if you want. If you don't know what to say, sit for a while in God's loving presence. If your mind wanders, don't worry; just bring yourself back to God's presence.

(Pause for a few minutes.)

Leader And now, think about anything that's happening in your own life that God or his angels might be able to help you with. Is there anything you want to change? Maybe it's an idea you had about angels and what they are. Or maybe it's about some fear you've had. Take a few minutes now and decide what you want to do.

(Pause briefly.)

Leader Our meditation is coming to a close, so take a minute to thank God for his presence. And then slowly open your eyes. In the name of the Father, and of the Son, and of the Holy Spirit. Amen.

Nine to one: A one-day novena*

ST. THÉRÈSE OF LISIEUX, OCTOBER 1

WHAT YOU'LL NEED

- **Bible**
- **candle**
- **flowers**—*as many different kinds as you can find (optional)*

THINGS TO DO AHEAD OF TIME

- *Familiarize your students with St. Thérèse of Lisieux. Suggest her autobiography, **The Story of a Soul**, to anyone who shows particular interest. You can also find her story on the Internet. A good place to start is **www.littleflower.org**.*

- *Print and distribute the novena to your students.*

f there's any saint who understands middle schoolers, it's St. Thérèse. Her struggles, disappointments, and hidden life reflect universal adolescent issues. Her "little way" of small deeds has resonated with believers around the world. Yet she received no special favors from God. As the theologian Michael Novak writes, "It is wrong to imagine that Thérèse constantly experienced burning ardor....She didn't. She spent years in darkness, seeing what you and I see, ordinary things, and of God nothing at all" ("St. Thérèse, Doctor of the Church," *Crisis* [December 1997]).

Encourage your students to learn more about the life of this saint—they might see a reflection of their own.

A Novena? Seriously?
A novena is a series of prayers, usually said on nine successive days. Since many classes don't meet for nine days in a row, this prayer service can be done in one meeting. If you don't have time to say all the prayers, break your class into small groups, and have each group say one or two of the prayers simultaneously.

Nine to one: A one-day novena

Light a candle. Everyone can stay in their places or find a comfortable spot in the prayer corner.

Leader Today, we're going to break the rules a little. We're saying a prayer called a novena. These prayers usually take nine days, but we don't have that much time. So we're doing it all in one day. Our novena prayer is to St. Thérèse of Lisieux. Thérèse died when she was only 24 years old, but she said, "I will spend my heaven doing good upon earth." So let's ask her to do some good for us right now. In the name of the Father, and of the Son, and of the Holy Spirit.

Thérèse, during your short life, you had to deal with a lot. Listen to our prayers, Thérèse, and please send them to Jesus.

FIRST PRAYER

Reader Thérèse, I have days when I feel like I can't do anything right.

Help me turn those days over to Jesus. Help me see that everything I do, even the mistakes I make, are part of God's plan. Help me see that he loves me, mistakes and all.

All Jesus, I believe in you. Strengthen my faith. Increase my love for you and for everyone. Don't ever let me lose hope in your mercy and love.

SECOND PRAYER

Reader Thérèse, there are times when I look forward to something that doesn't happen. It's so incredibly disappointing. So help me with my patience, because I may not be able to see the good in this for a long time. Help me keep going, even when I don't want to.

All Jesus, I believe in you. Strengthen my faith. Increase my love for you and for everyone. Don't ever let me lose hope in your mercy and love.

THIRD PRAYER

Reader Thérèse, sometimes I feel like people criticize me, or say terrible things about me all day long. Help me put the negative stuff out of my mind. Keep me from returning the mean words. Help me remember Jesus on the cross, who said, "Father, forgive them, because they don't know what they're doing."

All Jesus, I believe in you. Strengthen my faith. Increase my love for you and for everyone. Don't ever let me lose hope in your mercy and love.

FOURTH PRAYER

Reader Thérèse, sometimes I feel really alone. I'm pretty sure you know how I feel, because you lost your mother when you were four years old. Then your older sister left home to join the convent. Your world sort of crashed down on you. Show me that Jesus understands all of this too. Help me cope. Help me find my friend Jesus in the silence.

All Jesus, I believe in you. Strengthen my faith. Increase my love for you and for everyone. Don't ever let me lose hope in your mercy and love.

FIFTH PRAYER

Reader Thérèse, sometimes I feel like I really don't belong anywhere. One day people tell me I'm too young for things. The next day they tell me I need to grow up and be mature. Help me look to Jesus for courage to get through this time. O Jesus, I believe in you. Strengthen my faith. Increase my love for you and for everyone. Don't ever let me lose hope in your mercy and love.

All Jesus, I believe in you. Strengthen my faith. Increase my love for you and for everyone. Don't ever let me lose hope in your mercy and love.

SIXTH PRAYER

Reader Thérèse, sometimes it feels like God isn't listening to my prayers, and I can't find him. You had days like this. How did you do it? Help me keep going. Help me find the peace of knowing God's amazing love is always with me, even if I don't feel it.

All Jesus, I believe in you. Strengthen my faith. Increase my love for you and for everyone. Don't ever let me lose hope in your mercy and love.

SEVENTH PRAYER

Reader Thérèse, I see a lot of suffering and pain in this world. I don't understand it. Sometimes the people I love suffer. Sometimes I have to deal with pain. Help me, Thérèse. Help us all. Help me see that Jesus suffered because he loves me. Help me understand that when I suffer, I'm with Jesus, even if I don't know it. Help me get through the pain without complaining. And give me compassion for others who suffer too.

All Jesus, I believe in you. Strengthen my faith. Increase my love for you and for everyone. Don't ever let me lose hope in your mercy and love.

EIGHTH PRAYER

Reader Thérèse, sometimes I feel really small and unwanted. When you felt this way, you said it was a grace, and a victory. It was your way of serving God. You called it "your little way." Thérèse, can you teach me this? Can you show me how I can serve God this way? Can you show me the joy that comes in feeling small and unimportant? Because I'd really like to understand this.

All Jesus, I believe in you. Strengthen my faith. Increase my love for you and for everyone. Don't ever let me lose hope in your mercy and love.

NINTH PRAYER

Reader Thérèse, you know how it feels to be really happy one day, and incredibly sad the next. You understand how it feels to lose control of your emotions, even when you promise yourself you won't. Help me deal with these crazy feelings.

All Jesus, I believe in you. Strengthen my faith. Increase my love for you and for everyone. Don't ever let me lose hope in your mercy and love.

Leader It's said that those who pray with faith in God through Thérèse will find roses. Maybe it's in the smile of someone who's usually mean. Maybe it's a real rose that someone gives us. Let's look for these roses this week as we look for Jesus in our lives.

St. Therese, pray for us. In the name of the Father, and of the Son, and of the Holy Spirit. Amen.

Christ in the mirror

ST. TERESA OF AVILA, OCTOBER 15

WHAT YOU'LL NEED

■ **small mirror** *to pass among the group*

■ **copies of the prayer of St. Teresa of Avila** *(see the Handout section, page 134, or give students a prayer card of your own)*

The famous prayer of St. Teresa of Avila is adapted here for middle schoolers.

Christic in the mirror

Gather in a prayer circle.

All   In the name of the Father, and of the Son, and of the Holy Spirit. Amen.

Leader   Jesus, we can't see you on this earth the way your apostles did, but there's still a way…

(Invite everyone to look at their hands for a moment or two.)

Leader   The hands you're seeing are the hands of Jesus. And no. I'm not crazy. It's a theological truth.

(Invite everyone to look at their feet for a moment or two.)

Leader   The feet you're seeing are the feet of Jesus. Really. I know you don't believe me, but it's true.

(Pass around the mirror and invite everyone to look at their reflection.)

Leader   The eyes you see are the eyes of Christ. I'm not making this up. If you don't believe me, then read this prayer.

(Distribute the prayer of St. Teresa of Avila, and invite everyone to read it together.)

Leader   So, Jesus, give our hands the strength to do your work. Help them feed the poor. Shelter the homeless. Welcome the unwanted. And at the end of the day, bring them together in prayer.
     Help our feet walk in your footsteps. And when we're tired and we need rest, give us peace and comfort with you.
     Help us see you in every person we meet. In the name of the Father, and of the Son, and of the Holy Spirit. Amen.

It's all good

ST. FRANCIS OF ASSISI, OCTOBER 4

**THINGS TO DO
AHEAD OF TIME**

[OPTIONAL]

■ *This prayer service lends itself to a slide presentation. Search the Internet for photos of inspiring images of nature to use throughout this prayer. (Make sure any images you use are in the public domain and that you are allowed to copy them.) If you don't have the time or inclination to create a slide show, simply ask students to close their eyes and picture some of the sites you describe.*

Many parishes have a Blessing of the Animals on the feast of St. Francis. But why limit blessings to the animal kingdom? Use this prayer service to honor all of God's creation, as St. Francis did.

It's all good

As you gather, sing or play a recording of an appropriate song, such as "Awesome God" by Rich Mullins. Keep the song playing softly throughout the prayer celebration.

All In the name of the Father, and the Son, and of the Holy Spirit. Amen.

Leader Our response today is, "It's all good. Because you created it, Lord."
Lord, we see your wondrous creation. We see galaxies and stars, spreading across space like sand sparkling on the seashore. Our brains can't comprehend this endless space, but you *made* infinity. That's how incredible your creation is.

All It's all good. Because you created it, Lord.

Leader Lord, we see the wide, deep oceans. Scientists tell us that if we scoop up one small cup of water, we hold in our hands a number of molecules that's greater than all the gallons of water in all the oceans combined. That's how incredible your creation is.

All It's all good. Because you created it, Lord.

Leader We see the creatures of the earth, Lord. They have grown and adapted perfectly to where they live. An arctic wolf. An African elephant. A desert roadrunner. That's how incredible your creation is.

All It's all good. Because you created it, Lord

Leader We see our families, Lord. We see our friends, the people around us. We see ourselves. Different in many ways, but all created in your image. That's how incredible your creation is.

All It's all good. Because you created it, Lord.

Leader O God, everything you create is good because you're good. And that means we're good too. We're all part of your good creation. That's why Saint Francis called everything family: Brother Sun and Sister Moon; Brother Wind and Sister Water. So we join brother Francis as we say his prayer:

All Praise and bless my Lord and give him thanks. Serve him with great humility. In the name of the Father, and of the Son, and of the Holy Spirit.

A litany of saints, sort of

ALL SAINTS, NOVEMBER 1

The Litany of the Saints is one of the oldest group prayers in the church. It's also one of the longest. Try this variation to suit middle school attention spans.

THINGS TO DO AHEAD OF TIME
[OPTIONAL]

■ *Write down the names of some saints on slips of paper. (You can use the handout "Saints Who Fascinate Us," page 134.)*

■ *Or collect several saint holy cards. Place the holy cards or slips of paper in a basket or other container.*

■ *Choose two readers and make copies of the Introduction Dialogue (page 34) for them.*

FOLLOW UP

After you've finished the prayer service, provide some class time for students to research their saint.

For your students with smart phones, allow them to search the name of the saint they've chosen. Others can use your classroom computer, if it's got an Internet connection. Or provide some "Lives of the Saints" books and biographies for them to browse through.

If you can, find some "saintly" music to play as background, such as "Saints of God" by Bob Hurd or "For All the Saints" by Ralph Vaughan Williams.

A litany of saints (sort of)

Reader 1 So today, we're supposed to be learning about great Catholic saints.

But here's the thing. It's hard being Catholic, let alone being a saint. We see people around us all the time who don't do very saintly things and yet call themselves Catholics, or Christians. So what can we do about it?

Reader 2 I think we all know where this is going. I bet we're supposed to pray for those people, right? Nobody's perfect, I guess.

Reader 1 That's true, but there must be something else.

Reader 2 Um, let's see. We can…go to church?

Reader 1 Oh yeah. You know the Eucharist is a sign of Jesus' complete love for us. Every time we receive him, we get new strength to deal with whatever comes our way.

Reader 2 Uh, yeah. That's right. Where did you learn that?

Reader 1 No idea. I'm just reading it on the sheet. But it's true, isn't it?

Reader 2 Yeah. I guess you're right. What else have you got?

Reader 1 Uh, well, we can rely on God's grace. There's a lot of stuff in this world that doesn't make sense. So we have to trust in God's will that somehow it will all work out in the end. That's what the saints did.

Reader 2 Wow. Again, how do you know this?

Reader 1 You do realize I'm reading all this, don't you? It's on your sheet too. How are you missing this? But anyway, we can learn a lot from the saints, and how they dealt with people and events.

Reader 2 Right.

Reader 1 You're still not getting this, are you? Let's just move on to the next part.

Leader We think of saints as people who had all the answers, but most of the time, they had no idea how to deal with their problems. And things often went terribly wrong for them, or so it seemed at the time. But they always trusted God. So today we're going to ask for their help. Any place we've been, they've probably been there too.

(Invite everyone to select a name from the basket without looking. Don't forget to take one yourself.)

Leader In the name of the Father, and of the Son, and of the Holy Spirit.

All Amen.

Leader Lord God, your saints never knew what the future held, or what dangers were ahead of them. But they trusted you. Today we've been given the name of a saint we might not know. But we're going to trust that somehow, there's a reason for it.

(Invite each person to say the name of the saint they've chosen. The rest can respond with, "Pray for us." Then conclude with the following:)

Leader Today, Lord, we've each chosen a saint, but we realize it's entirely possible that they have chosen us. We may know very little about our saint. Maybe nothing. So we ask you, Lord, to search your heavens and bring these good people close to us. Ask them to watch over us, guide us, and keep us close to you.

Holy saints of God, pray for us.

All In the name of the Father, and of the Son, and of the Holy Spirit. Amen.

We honor the dead: A classroom shrine

THE COMMEMORATION OF ALL THE FAITHFUL DEPARTED (ALL SOULS), NOVEMBER 2

WHAT YOU'LL NEED

■ **Bible** or lectionary with the following readings noted: **Wisdom 3:1-3** and **John 11:25-26**

■ **candle** (optional)

■ **mementoes or photos** of the dead and/or **symbols** such as dried foliage (see "Create a Class Shrine," page 131)

THINGS TO DO AHEAD OF TIME

■ Choose some music (see suggestions on page 37).

■ Assign volunteer readers.

Whether they've experienced it through unwholesome or impersonal media images, or through the death of a family member, friend, or pet, middle schoolers are familiar with death. So don't be afraid of dealing with the subject head-on. By offering prayers for the dead throughout the month of November, show that our faith memory is neither fleeting nor impersonal. Provide a contrast to the media portrayals with the true reality of death: respect, honor, and dignity. In this way, students can see that each of us, as members of Christ's body, are on the same path toward his eternal kingdom of love, peace, and joy.

Honoring the dead

CLASSROOM SHRINE AND PRAYER SERVICE

Light a candle and gather around your shrine. Have everyone carry a memento, photo, or other symbol. Sing or play a recording of an appropriate song, such as "In Paradisum," or "I Am the Bread of Life" by Suzanne Toolan, RSM.

Leader In the name of the Father, and of the Son, and of the Holy Spirit.
All Amen.

Leader Jesus, today we gather around your holy cross to remember all those who have died. We begin by listening to your word.

Reader 1 *(Read Wisdom 3:1–3)*

Reader 2 *(Read John 11:25–26)*

Leader God of life, today we honor our friends, family, and all those we don't know who have left this world and entered your presence. We will never forget our beloved dead.

(As prayers are offered, invite students to bring their symbols to the prayer shrine.)

Leader Jesus, you died on the cross, and after three days you rose from the dead. Welcome everyone who follows you into their amazing new life with you. Please respond, "We will never forget."
All We will never forget.

Leader For all those who have died—those we know and those we don't know—we pray that they find rest in you.
All We will never forget.

Leader Today seems like it should be a sad day, Lord, but we remember that you are the resurrection and the life. Even though we die, we will live with you forever.
All We will never forget.

Leader We thank you for the gift of life, which we appreciate more than ever. We promise to live our lives with faith in you, and with love, mercy, and compassion toward all the living and the dead. In the name of the Father, the Son, and the Holy Spirit.
All Amen.

We honor the dead: A bulb planting memorial

THE COMMEMORATION OF ALL THE FAITHFUL DEPARTED (ALL SOULS), NOVEMBER 2

Here's an alternative approach to this feast day that focuses on new life.

WHAT YOU'LL NEED

- **flower bulbs**, one for each person
- **pots full of planting medium** or a patch of soil on your parish or school property (Be sure to get permission before you dig!)
- **small spades** or shovels
- **water source**/watering can
- **Bible** (open to John 11:17–27, 38–44)

THINGS TO DO AHEAD OF TIME

- Follow the directions on the bulb package for soil preparation. Your students can take care of all the soil preparation if you don't have time.

- If you are planting in pots, lay out plenty of newspaper on your work surface.

Honoring the dead

BULB PLANTING MEMORIAL

Gather in your planting area. Sing or play a recording of an appropriate song, such as "Because the Lord Is My Shepherd" by Christopher Walker or "On Eagle's Wings" by Michael Joncas.

Leader   In the name of the Father, and of the Son, and of the Holy Spirit.
We begin today with the word of the Lord.

(Read John 11:17–27)

Leader   Lord God of Life, today we plant these flower bulbs. We see that they are rough, brown, and, well, not pretty. It's hard to believe these dead-looking things will amount to much. Yet, inside of them is your gift of life. So bless these small bulbs. Bless the hands that plant them, in the name of the Father, and of the Son, and of the Holy Spirit.

As we plant these bulbs, we will read from the Psalms. When I pause, you can respond, "The Lord is my shepherd; there is nothing I lack."

(Have everyone plant the bulbs, while a leader or an assistant reads the prayer below, based on Psalm 23.)

Leader   The Lord is my shepherd; I lack nothing. He brings me to the most beautiful places, full of green grass and living water. He restores my soul.

All   The Lord is my shepherd; there is nothing I lack.

Leader   He guides me along all the right paths. Even though I walk through the valley of the shadow of death, I'm not afraid of any evil. Because God always walks with me.

All   The Lord is my shepherd; there is nothing I lack.

Leader   Your goodness and mercy follow me; I'll stay in the house of the Lord forever.

All   The Lord is my shepherd; there is nothing I lack.

(When the bulbs have been planted, begin the blessing over them.)

Leader   Lord God, we offer these bulbs to you. For a long time they'll lie here in the frozen, dark earth. When we look out here, we may not see anything, but you give us hope. Let's listen to more of the Gospel.

(Read John 11:38–44)

Leader   Lord Jesus, as we look at the brown earth, we know that these bulbs will one day be like Lazarus, full of life and newness. And one day we too will be resurrected, through your own death and resurrection. So now we say,

All   Our Father, who art in heaven...
In the name of the Father, and of the Son, and of the Holy Spirit. Amen.

(Proceed back inside to the accompaniment of a sung or recorded hymn.)

Thanksgiving shout-out

WHAT YOU'LL NEED

- **poster board**
- **markers**

Y ou can use this prayer at Thanksgiving, or any time you want to help your students develop grateful hearts. Earplugs are optional.

THINGS TO DO AHEAD OF TIME

■ *Write "Thanks for everything, God" on the poster boards, and place them on walls or easels around your learning space.*

■ *At the beginning of class, give everyone some time to write down things they are thankful for. Keep the boards up throughout the class, and allow for time throughout your session for students to add items. (You may even want to leave the posters up over the course of a few lessons.)*

■ *To keep this from getting completely out of hand, set aside two poster boards that are JUST SILLY. Students can write whatever silly things they want to thank God for (no profanities, of course) as long as they write three serious things they're thankful for on the other poster boards first.*

■ *When you're ready, collect the posters and place them in and around your prayer table.*

■ *Choose a reader or two for the psalm.*

Thanksgiving shout-out

As you gather, sing or play a recording of a song of thanks, such as "All Good Gifts" by Kevin Keil, "All My Days" by Dan Schutte, or "Blessed Be Your Name" by Matt Redman and Beth Redman.

Leader Lord God, we thank you today, tomorrow, and always for your countless blessings. We gather here to offer you a psalm of praise* for all these gifts you have showered on us. Let's say the psalm refrain together:

All Give thanks to the Lord for he is good; his mercy endures forever.

Reader Let everyone say it. His love lasts forever.
Let everyone shout it. His love lasts forever.
Let everyone who respects the Lord sing it. His love lasts forever.

All Give thanks to the Lord for he is good; his mercy endures forever.

Reader I thank you, God, because you answered me; you are my savior.
Even when everything looks bad,
Even when everyone rejects me,
You are at my side. You do everything for me. It is wonderful in my eyes.

All Give thanks to the Lord for he is good; his mercy endures forever.

Reader This is the day the Lord has made; so let's be happy.
Let's celebrate. Let's shout.

All Give thanks to the Lord for he is good; his mercy endures forever.

Leader No, really. Let's shout it as loud as we can:

All Give thanks to the Lord for he is good; his mercy endures forever.

Leader I'm not sure they heard you back at your house. Let's do it again.

All Give thanks to the Lord for he is good; his mercy endures forever.

Leader *(quietly)* Thank you.
In the name of the Father, and of the Son, and of the Holy Spirit.

All Amen.

Based on Psalm 118

Four for faith

ADVENT WREATH WEEKLY PRAYER SERVICES
WEEK 1: A LIGHT IN THE DARKNESS

WHAT YOU'LL NEED

- **Advent wreath**
- **candles**
- **Bible** or lectionary

(open to Isaiah 60:1–3)

ABOUT ADVENT WREATHS You can put together an Advent wreath with any kind of budget. Whether it's store bought or homemade, with craft store greenery or live branches from the garden, your Advent wreath should be the focal point of your classroom decorating in December. You'll use four candles: three purple and one pink. The most important thing to keep in mind is candle safety. Make sure they can't easily tip over, and never leave them unattended.

If anyone needs Advent it's middle schoolers. So resist the temptation to light a candle at the beginning of class and move on to an unrelated lesson plan. Allow the season to wrap you in its graces. Let it spill into everything you do, so your students begin to feel that joyful hope and blessed anticipation of our Savior, and our true life.

The Church gives us themes for each week of Advent. Keep these themes in mind as you plan your lessons:

WEEK 1: Hope | **WEEK 2:** Peace | **WEEK 3:** Joy | **WEEK 4:** Love

THINGS TO DO AHEAD OF TIME

■ *Rest the Bible on a table or other platform near the Advent wreath.*

■ *Assign four volunteers to read the various parts. Explain how the readings will take place: The class will process in and stand in a circle around the Advent wreath and the Bible, with the four readers standing closest to the Bible. After the first candle is lit, Reader 1 will come forward and read by the light of the candle, then move back to his or her place in the circle, followed by Reader 2, and so forth.*

■ *Clear a path (Advent pun intended) for a procession to your Advent wreath. Remember you will be in darkness or semi-darkness, so watch for obstructions like backpack straps or books.*

A light in the darkness

ADVENT WEEK 1 PRAYER SERVICE

Turn down the lights in your learning space, and invite everyone to stand and form a single line in the back. Begin the hymn and lead your class in procession; then gather in a circle around the wreath. When the hymn ends, wait for silence, and begin.

Leader In the name of the Father, and of the Son, and of the Holy Spirit.
All Amen.

In silence light the first purple candle of the Advent wreath. Leave the script near the candle so that the readers may come up to read it.

Reader 1 One candle. One light in the darkness.

Reader 2 One star. One light in the night sky.

Reader 3 One baby. One savior born into a world of sin and despair.

Reader 4 One hope. In Jesus Christ, who shatters the power of sin and sadness forever.

Leader Now let's listen as the word of God is proclaimed.

(Read Isaiah 60: 1–3)

Leader Today, we light this one candle as a symbol of our hope in the one savior, Jesus, who comes to conquer the darkness of fear and sin. But our candle doesn't make the whole room bright. We have to come forward to see. Just as we are called to come forward into the light of Jesus' love.

(Turn up the lights.)

Leader Let's respond with the words of the prophet Isaiah, "The people who walked in darkness have seen a great light."

All The people who walked in darkness have seen a great light.

Leader Father in heaven, today we really have walked in darkness. But one small candle gives us hope in your great Light. The Light that comes to save us from the darkness. The Light that is your Son. Emmanuel. God-With-Us.

All The people who walked in darkness have seen a great light.

Leader In the name of the Father, and of the Son, and of the Holy Spirit.

All Amen.

Four for faith

WEEK 2: WAKE UP!

WHAT YOU'LL NEED

- **Advent wreath**
- **candles**
- **Bible** *or lectionary*
(open to Matthew 3:1-6)

Rearranging your learning space probably doesn't seem like a very peaceful activity, especially in light of the week's theme of peace. But Advent is a dynamic time. A time to change, make amends, and move out of comfort zones. "Stay awake," Jesus says. "For you know neither the day nor the hour."

Still, you may wonder what that has to do with the theme of peace. As Mark tells us, "John the Baptizer appeared in the wilderness, preaching a baptism of repentance for the forgiveness of sins." Repentance and forgiveness are the only ways to the true peace of Jesus. In the Church's traditional prayer for the second week of Advent, we ask God to "stir up our hearts." That's our way to true peace.

THINGS TO DO AHEAD OF TIME

■ *Rest the Bible on a table or other platform near the Advent wreath.*

■ *Before class, rearrange the desks or tables in your learning space as much as you can. Move your Advent wreath and prayer table to another part of the classroom. Or place obstacles on the chairs—stacks of textbooks or boxes, for example. When your students arrive, welcome them, but don't explain things. Let the prayer service explain it for you.*

■ *Copy and print the Confiteor prayer (see Handout section, page 135), or provide missals for everyone to read.*

Wake up!

As you gather around your Advent wreath, sing or play a recording of an Advent song (not a Christmas carol). Some suggestions include "Find us Ready, Lord" by Tom Booth, "Ready the Way" by Curtis Stephan, or the traditional "O Come, O Come, Emmanuel." Everyone should remain standing until the Gospel passage is read.

Leader In the name of the Father, and of the Son, and of the Holy Spirit.

All Amen.

Leader Father in heaven, today we gather around our Advent wreath and we ask you to stir up our hearts. As we light these candles, make us ready for your Son, so that we can serve him always.

(Light the first and second purple Advent candles.)

Leader And now, let's listen to the Gospel.

Reader *(Read Matthew 3:1–6)*

(Invite everyone to be seated.)

Leader So take a look at the classroom again. How did it make you feel when you walked in here and saw what was going on?

(Pause for possible answers and brief discussion.)

Leader If you felt a little confused, imagine how the people of John the Baptist's time felt. John wanted people to change. He wanted to make them uncomfortable. Why?

(Pause for possible answers and brief discussion.)

Leader Let's pray about this. Lord, our learning space looks and feels different, but it's what John the Baptist wants. If he were living today, he'd tell us to stop sitting around like couch potatoes. He'd tell us to get moving and change our ways. So in your presence we think about what we need to change in our lives.

(*Pause briefly.*) For all those times we've sinned against God and against each other, let's pray for forgiveness—from God and from those around us.

(Say the Confiteor prayer together.)

Leader And because the whole point of this is to get to Jesus' peace, let's offer each other a sign of Christ's peace.

(Invite everyone to greet each other with, "Peace be with you.")

Leader Lord God, keep guiding us through this Advent season. Forgive our sins, and help us forgive others too. We ask you this through your Son, our Lord Jesus Christ, Emmanuel, God-With-Us.

In the name of the Father, and of the Son, and of the Holy Spirit.

All Amen.

Four for faith

WEEK 3: LET IT SHINE

WHAT YOU'LL NEED

- **paper or foam star cutouts**
(use those with a sticker backing;
otherwise, provide glue sticks)
- **large star** (cut from poster
board)
- **dark blue butcher paper**
(or painted deep blue to represent
the night sky)
- **pens** or markers
- **Bible** or lectionary
(open to Luke 1:26–33)

The third Sunday of Advent, known as Gaudete Sunday, is just the remedy for the winter doldrums. The message is, Rejoice! We're almost there! As if in defiance of winter's gloom, everything at Mass brightens. The somber, deep violet of the vestments and altar cloths gives way to a brilliant rose. Flowers appear on the altar. And stars can twinkle in your classroom.

THINGS TO DO AHEAD OF TIME

- *Mount a picture or image of Jesus on the large star. Write "We follow the star" beneath the picture of Jesus. Mount the star on the butcher paper "night sky" and hang it on a wall or bulletin board. Clear a path (there's that Advent pun again) to your Advent wreath. Before class, scatter the star cutouts along the path.*

Let it shine

ADVENT WEEK 3 PRAYER SERVICE

Sing or play a recording of an Advent song. Suggestions include "We Shall Be The Light" by Mark Friedman and Janet Vogt, "Go Light Your World" by Chris Rice, or the traditional "O Come, O Come, Emmanuel." As students process in, invite them to pick up the stars in their path. Make sure everyone gets at least one.

Leader   In the name of the Father, and of the Son, and of the Holy Spirit.

All   Amen.

Leader   Father in heaven, today we gather around our Advent wreath in great joy. A few weeks ago, our space was lit by one tiny candle, but now the light has grown. Just as our joy grows in you during Advent.

As we light these candles, prepare our hearts. Help those who are feeling sad today so that they know the joy of your love.

(Light the first and second purple candles, and the third pink candle.)

Leader   And now, let's listen to the word of the Lord.

Reader   *(Read Luke 1:26–33)*

Leader   Some people say they don't believe in you because they can't see you.

Help us to be signs for them, Lord. Maybe there's a loner at school we can talk to. Maybe we can collect food for the poor over the break. There are hundreds of ways we can be signs of your love.

(Invite students to close their eyes and think of ways they will be signs of God during Advent. When they're ready, tell them to write what they plan to do on their stars, and place them on the "night sky." As students write on the stars, play a recording of an Advent song. When they've finished, have them make the Sign of the Cross.)

Four for faith

WEEK 4: A MOM'S LOVE

WHAT YOU'LL NEED

▪ **statue or image of Mary**
(place the image near your Advent wreath)
▪ **baby blanket**
▪ **Bible** *or lectionary*
(open to Luke 1:39-45)

THINGS TO DO AHEAD OF TIME

▪ *Inspect your Advent wreath and give it a dusting or final sprucing up in this last week before Christmas. Enlist students to help, if you want.*

▪ *Assign some readers for the prayers.*

Who better to show us this week's Advent theme of love than a mom? If you weren't able to celebrate any of December's Marian feasts, here's an opportunity to honor our Blessed Mother.

A mom's love

ADVENT WEEK 4 PRAYER SERVICE

Sing or play a recording of a Marian hymn as you gather around your Advent wreath. "Be With Us, Mary" by Tom Booth is especially appropriate for Advent. Pass around the baby blanket and let everyone feel its softness. Then place it in your prayer corner or near your Advent wreath, and light all four candles.

Leader In the name of the Father, and of the Son, and of the Holy Spirit.

All Amen.

Leader O Lord, today we think about Mary getting ready for your son's birth. It's not like she could run to Target or Wal-Mart for everything. She had to make blankets and swaddling clothes herself. It took a lot of patience and prayer. So we bring this blanket to our prayer celebration, to remind us not to "harden our hearts" to your voice. Help us remember Mary's gentle love and incredible courage as we listen to her story.

Reader 1 *(Read Luke 1:39–45)*

Reader 2 O Lord, after everything the angel told her, Mary could have spent this time taking care of her own needs. And that would have been fine. But she left her home to help her cousin Elizabeth. Help us think of others this week, especially those who are unable to ask for help.

Let's respond, "If today you hear his voice, harden not your hearts."

All If today you hear his voice, harden not your hearts.

Reader 3 O Lord, when Mary visited Elizabeth, she could have spent the whole time talking about her fears and worries. And that would have been understandable. Instead, she sang a song of praise to you. Help us remember that all good gifts come from you alone. Help us remember to pray.

All If today you hear his voice, harden not your hearts.

Reader 4 O Lord God, when Mary heard your voice, she could have hardened her heart and said no. It would have been understandable; after all, you were asking a lot. But she opened her heart to you, totally and completely. So, Lord, this is a tough one. Can you open our hearts, minds, and souls to you? We ask your help, in the name of your Son, our Lord Jesus Christ, who loves us now and always.

In the name of the Father, and of the Son, and of the Holy Spirit. Amen.

Service project blessing

ST. NICHOLAS, DECEMBER 6

WHAT YOU'LL NEED

■ **image of St. Nicholas**
(optional)

■ **Bible** or lectionary
(open to Matthew 19:16–22)

THINGS TO DO AHEAD OF TIME

■ *Find an image of St. Nicholas and add it to your prayer corner. Check http://www. stnicholascenter.org for images and activities.*

■ *Select a volunteer for the reading.*

■ *Print out the blessing prayer on pages 54-55 for all to say together.*

Some of your students may be familiar with the St. Nicholas Day custom of hiding treats in shoes. Adapt this tradition to a middle school audience by developing an Advent service project in honor of St. Nicholas. Whether you start a collection for the poor (a shoe drive might be appropriate), or you volunteer in a soup kitchen, ask for St. Nicholas' blessing before beginning your outreach activities. This service is appropriate during Advent but can be adapted for use throughout the year.

Saint Nicholas service project blessing

Gather in your prayer corner. Sing or play a recording of a song such as "The Cry of the Poor" by John Foley, SJ or "We Are Called" by David Haas.

Leader   In the name of the Father, and of the Son, and of the Holy Spirit. Amen.

Reader   *(Read Matthew 19:16–22)*

Leader   Let's think about this. What is it that makes the young man so sad?

(Pause for reflection. If needed, quietly reread the passage. Allow students to share any thoughts or ideas.)

Leader   Is Jesus asking us to give all of our possessions away?

(Pause again for reflection. Allow students to share any thoughts or ideas.)

Leader   The young man wants to be closer to God, but money gets in the way. And it makes him sad. Is there anything that gets in between God and me? Let's think about that.

(Pause again for reflection. Allow students to share any thoughts or ideas.)

Leader   Today, we're focusing on other people. When we remember that Jesus is there in every person we meet, it makes sense that helping others is a way to get closer to him. That's exactly what St. Nicholas did. So let's thank God for this opportunity to help others. Maybe today is God's way of helping us get past whatever separates us from him. Let's pray together:

All Hey, Jesus, we're a little like the rich young man in the gospel because we're putting something between us and you. But in our case, we're hoping it actually brings us closer to you, because today we're serving others. Maybe our work today will bring others closer to you too. Maybe it will be a win-win situation.

Left Side Hey, Jesus, we're a little like St. Nicholas too, because we want to help others. We've heard legends and stories about him, but the truth is that he was a bishop who spent his entire life helping the poor, especially kids. By putting others first, he didn't let anything get in the way of his relationship with you. Help us follow St. Nicholas' example of faith, love, and kindness to all.

Right Side Hey, Jesus, help us remember why we're doing this today. It's not to make us feel good about ourselves (even though we'll probably feel good anyway). It's about loving you and loving our neighbor, pure and simple. The same way that St. Nicholas did. So bless our work this day. Bless anyone who benefits from what we do. May it lead them, and us, to you.

All In the name of the Father, and of the Son, and of the Holy Spirit. Amen.

¡Viva la Virgen de Guadalupe!

OUR LADY OF GUADALUPE, DECEMBER 12

THINGS TO DO AHEAD OF TIME

◼ *If your students aren't familiar with the beautiful lady who appeared to Juan Diego in Mexico in 1531, this is a good time to introduce her. You can find several Internet resources and books, including **The Lady of Guadalupe** by Tomie dePaola. (Yes, it's a children's picture book, but it's suitable for all ages.)*

◼ *Get your students involved in the planning. Have them decorate Our Lady's image with flowers and candles.*

◼ *Choose students to lead the rosary prayers.*

The feast of Our Lady of Guadalupe, *Nuestra Señora de Guadalupe*, is important to millions of Americans of Mexican heritage, but celebrations of the patroness of the Americas cross cultural boundaries. For those who celebrate it, December 12 is everything a feast day should be, including early morning candlelight processions, the singing of "Las Mañanitas" (a birthday song that's sung to Our Lady on this day), and sometimes even fireworks.

OK, so maybe you don't have a budget for *folklorico* dancers and *mariachi* music, but you can adapt the prayers, colors, and even Juan Diego's *tilma* to a classroom scale. The prayer service script is very basic, but you can add to it with the ideas and suggestions on page 57 or come up with your own ideas.

WHAT YOU'LL NEED

◼ *What you'll need depends on how big a celebration you want. Certainly it helps to begin with the image of Our Lady of Guadalupe. Check Catholic gift shops or print out a copy of her image from the Internet.*

Music

Recordings of "Las Mañanitas" are easy to find on the Internet. This is a joyful, festive song, but it's played at secular birthday celebrations, so be sure you find a recording that's appropriate for school or church use.

Optional: If you or any of your students know this song, you can teach it to your class and sing it together in a procession.

You can also use a song in English: "Our Lady of Guadalupe" by Sarah Hart and Angus McDonell.

Optional ideas

Decorations

- Use red roses or red poinsettias. Your class can create paper roses out of tissue paper and pipe cleaners and place them at the image.
- Although the liturgical colors for today are purple for Advent or white for a Marian feast, you can still decorate your prayer corner and your classroom in the vibrant colors of Mexico. Or place the image on blue fabric to represent Our Lady's mantle of stars. Have your students cover the mantle with gold star stickers.
- Votive candles are the the order of the day. Use the colors of Mexico: red, white, and green. Or find inexpensive Our Lady of Guadalupe candles in the ethnic food sections of your local grocery store. Use candles in a procession if you want.
- Display the flags of the Americas (Canada, the U.S., and Mexico) in your learning space to show Our Lady's patronage.

Activities

- Some people recreate the miraculous *tilma* of Juan Diego by photocopying the image of Our Lady and gluing it on some rough cotton fabric like linen or muslin.
- After your prayer celebration, have some fun by breaking open a *piñata*.
- Teach the Hail Mary in Spanish. (See Handout section, page 135.)

Procession

- It's not uncommon to see people crawling on their knees to the Basilica of Our Lady of Guadalupe in Mexico, symbolizing their penitence and humility. Invite your students to kneel and move toward the image on their knees at some point in your prayer service if you want.

Food

- Traditional foods served on this day include *tamales* (a mixture of meat and vegetables wrapped in *masa*, a corn meal dough, and boiled in corn husks), *pan dulce* (sweet bread), and *champurrado* (Mexican hot chocolate). You can find *pan dulce* in the ethnic section of most supermarkets, and most of your students won't say no to any kind of hot chocolate.

¡Viva la Virgen de Guadalupe!

OUR LADY OF GUADALUPE, DECEMBER 12

Process as a group to the image of Our Lady of Guadalupe, to the accompaniment of a Marian hymn or "Las Mañanitas."

Leader In the name of the Father, and of the Son, and of the Holy Spirit.
All Amen.

Leader Our response today is, *¡Viva la Virgen de Guadalupe!*
All ¡Viva la Virgen de Guadalupe! (VEE-vah la VEER-hane Deh Gwa-dah-LOO-peh)

Leader O God, Father of all kindness, you have given us your Son's most holy Mother, the Blessed Virgin of Guadalupe, to protect us and keep us firm in our faith.
All ¡Viva la Virgen de Guadalupe!

Leader O God, watch over us and guide us in the ways of justice and peace. Through our Lord Jesus Christ, your Son, who lives and reigns with you and the Holy Spirit, one God, forever and ever.
All ¡Viva la Virgen de Guadalupe!

Leader And now, let's listen to the Gospel of the Lord.

Reader 1 (*Read Luke 1:39–47*)
All ¡Viva la Virgen de Guadalupe!

Leader When Our Lady appeared to Juan Diego, she gave him signs, like the miraculous image on his *tilma*, to help him understand that she was the mother of God. But what's also amazing is that Our Lady appeared to Juan Diego in a way that was familiar to him. And she spoke his own Aztec dialect. This reminds us that God really wants us to understand him. He tells us never to be afraid. So let's say the words of Our Lady to Juan Diego.
All Let not your heart be disturbed...

Girls Am I not here, who am your Mother? Are you not under my protection? Am I not your health? Are you not happily within my fold?

Guys What else do you wish? Do not grieve nor be disturbed by anything.

All This is God's message to all of us: Don't be afraid. ¡Viva la Virgen de Guadalupe!

Leader And now we pray, in honor of Our Lady of Guadalupe, a decade of the rosary.

Student Leader Glory be to the Father, and to the Son and to the Holy Spirit.

All As it was in the beginning, is now, and ever shall be, world without end. Amen.

O my Jesus, forgive us our sins, save us from the fires of hell, lead all souls to heaven, especially those most in need of your mercy.

Student Leader Our Father, who art in heaven, hallowed be thy name. Thy kingdom come. Thy will be done on earth, as it is in heaven.

All Give us this day our daily bread and forgive us our trespasses as we forgive those who trespass against us; and lead us not into temptation, but deliver us from evil. Amen.

Student Leader Hail Mary, full of grace, the Lord is with thee. Blessed art thou among women, and blessed is the fruit of thy womb, Jesus.

All Holy Mary, Mother of God, pray for us sinners, now, and at the hour of our death. Amen.

(Say nine more Hail Marys, followed by a Glory be.)

All Hail, holy Queen, Mother of mercy, hail, our life, our sweetness, and our hope. To thee do we cry, poor banished children of Eve: to thee do we send up our sighs, mourning and weeping in this vale of tears. Turn then, most gracious Advocate, thine eyes of mercy toward us, and after this our exile, show unto us the blessed fruit of thy womb, Jesus. O clement, O loving, O sweet Virgin Mary!

Student Leader Pray for us, O holy mother of God.

All That we may be made worthy of the promises of Christ.

Student Leader In the name of the Father, and of the Son, and of the Holy Spirit.

All Amen.

Is this the place?

A NATIVITY SCENE BLESSING

WHAT YOU'LL NEED

■ **Nativity scene**

■ **Bible** *or lectionary with the following readings noted:* ***Luke 2:1-7, Luke 2:11-12, Luke 2:8-14, Luke 2:15-20***

THINGS TO DO AHEAD OF TIME

■ *Assign reading parts. If students will be placing the pieces and figures into the manger scene, assign each person to an object prior to the prayer service, to eliminate any confusion during prayer.*

■ *Print and copy the Blessing for your students to read.*

Appeal to middle schoolers' budding sense of rebellion by showing them that "old school" nativity scenes may be lovely, but the reality was probably pretty harsh.

Setting up a nativity scene in your classroom doesn't need to be expensive. You can even find nativity scene art on the Internet. Print the images, cut them out, and paste them to a cardboard backing. Add a support at the base, and you've got a homemade nativity scene to rival anything you'd find at a department store.

Involve all of your students in its creation and assembly with this simple prayer service. With several readings, you can involve almost everyone, and students who don't want to read aloud can place the figures in the scene as each section is read.

Is this the place?

A NATIVITY SCENE BLESSING

Gather around the place where you set up your nativity scene.

Leader   In the name of the Father, and of the Son, and of the Holy Spirit.
Lord Jesus, bless the scene we're recreating here. May it remind us that you, who
are God and creator of all things, became man here in the humblest of places.
Help us picture it in our minds as we ask, is this the place?

Reader 1   *(Read Luke 2:1–7)*

Reader 2   Is this the place? Mary and Joseph probably thought it was, at first. And who
wouldn't? It was the inn at Bethlehem, "the place to be" for travelers. The problem
was, everyone else in the city thought it was the place too. Anybody who was
somebody had gathered there. So for Mary and Joseph, "there was no room in
the inn." And now look. The most popular place in the city, that inn, is forgotten
today. We don't put it in our scene because no one cares.

Reader 3   Jesus, we're starting to get it. The most popular places can come and go. The
trends, the things that are "hot" right now—they could be gone in a few years. We
think about the crowded inn for only a minute. We're more interested in another
place. A smaller, humbler, less flashy place. That's where things really happened.

*(Place the stable into your scene, and anything that goes with it: the manger [don't put Jesus in
yet], straw, and animals.)*

Reader 4   *(Read Luke 2:11–12)*

Reader 5   Is this the place? Is this all that Mary and Joseph could find? I mean, it's a
manger, in a stable. There was no heat, so it was probably freezing at night.
No electricity, either, so there was no light to see anything. No carpet, just a
dirt floor. And that meant bugs, probably. And there were animals, so yeah, it
probably smelled.

Reader 6   Jesus, thinking about all this makes us appreciate little things, like electricity,
heating, a decent roof, and a clean floor. Looking at the manger full of hay makes
us take a look at our own beds, pillows, and blankets. It makes us think about

people who don't have any of that. So, Jesus, we ask you today to watch over all those who are homeless. Help them find a place to stay that's warm and safe.

(Place Mary and Joseph in the scene.)

Reader 7   *(Read Luke 2:8–14)*

Reader 8   Is this the place? You have to wonder what the shepherds thought. I mean, the angels made it sound like a big deal. They said, "A savior has been born for you, who is Messiah and Lord." You have to wonder if the shepherds thought they were going to a palace or something. And here's the Messiah, in a stable.

Reader 9   Jesus, did the shepherds care that you were born in a stable? Sounds like they couldn't have cared less. All they could think about was how amazing everything was. Did the angels care? Sounds like they were overjoyed, dancing and singing in the skies, "praising God and saying, 'Glory to God in the highest, and on earth peace to those on whom his favor rests.'"

(Place shepherds and angels in the scene.)

Reader 10   *(Read Luke 2:15–20)*

Reader 11   Is this the place? Amazing, isn't it? Here in a stable, the savior of the whole world. "All who heard it were amazed."

Reader 12   Lord Jesus, we're pretty amazed too. This really is something. Thanks for bringing us here to this place where you were born. Like Mary, we'll reflect on all these things. Like the shepherds, we'll glorify and praise God for this amazing gift, forever and ever.

All   In the name of the Father, and of the Son, and of the Holy Spirit. Amen.

Celebrating Christmas in January

FEAST OF THE EPIPHANY

WHAT YOU'LL NEED

■ **foil gift wrap** *in gold, purple, or red (cut into 3" x 5" pieces)*

■ **pens** *or markers*

■ **decorated gift boxes** *(optional)*

■ **Bible** *or lectionary (open to Matthew 2:1–6 and 7–12)*

■ **Twelfth Night cake** *or other baked goods (optional)*

■ **"Wassail" punch**—*use cider or juice (optional)*

THINGS TO DO AHEAD OF TIME

■ *Keep your Nativity scene up at least until this prayer celebration. Don't forget to add the baby Jesus to the manger if you haven't already.*

L et's face it. Middle schoolers won't be happy about returning to school after the Christmas break. So get their minds off the end of vacation with a noisy, raucous celebration. Also known as Twelfth Night or the Feast of the Three Kings, the Epiphany marks the culmination of the Christmas season, as Christ is revealed to the Gentiles through the Magi. Many European Christians reserve their biggest feasting and gift-giving for this day. Make this prayer service a celebration worthy of the King of Kings, with feasting, gifts, and—yes—fun.

THINGS TO DO ON THE DAY OF THE SERVICE

Give each person three squares of the gift wrap. On the "wrong" side, have them write three gifts they will give the Savior in the New Year. Have them fold the sheets and place them in the gift boxes (optional) to be placed at the Nativity scene when you process in.

Feeding those hungry middle schoolers

Twelfth Night cake, or King's cake (*roscón de reyes* in Spain), is a European tradition. Its ring shape represented the circular routes the Magi are said to have taken to find Jesus, to throw King Herod off their trail and thus thwart his plan to kill the Christ Child. A bean was baked into the fruitcake-like confection, and whoever bit into it was crowned king or queen of the day. Of course, food allergies and choking risk make the old version impossible these days, but the idea of enticing your middle schoolers back to class with baked goods isn't a bad idea. Forget adding the bean, but consider baking a ring-shaped cake (a Bundt cake) and having someone carry it in your procession.

Another tradition, wassail punch, is served on this day in England. Create your own updated nonalcoholic version with apple juice, hot mulled cider, or sparkling cider. Serve after the prayer celebration with Twelfth Night cake.

Optional Ideas

- Have everyone wear paper crowns (available at party supply stores) as you process into the classroom, in imitation of the Magi.
- Check the after-New-Year's sales for noisemakers, to use as a "kingly salute" to drive out the old year.

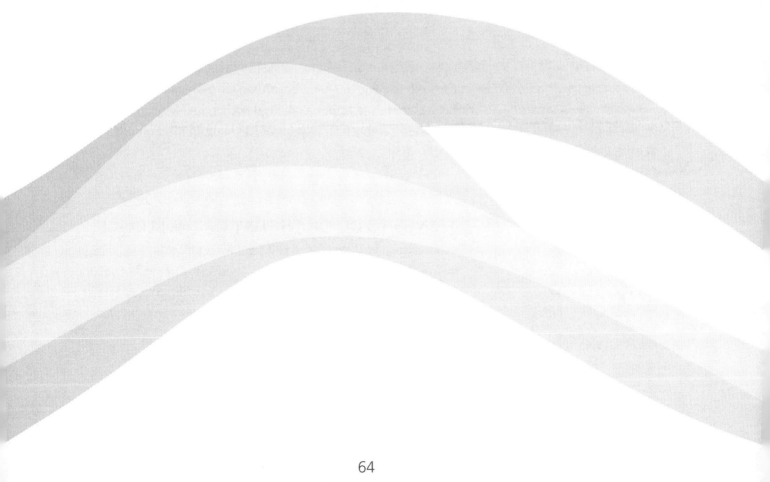

Celebrating Christmas in January

FEAST OF THE EPIPHANY

As your students arrive, greet them with Christmas carols and decorations. Allow some time for students to mingle and catch up with friends as they write their gifts on the foil squares. Then invite everyone to line up in a procession and bring their gifts to Jesus in the nativity scene. You might want to play a recording of "We Three Kings" at this point. Remain at the scene until the song ends.

Leader   In the name of the Father, and of the Son, and of the Holy Spirit.

All   Amen.

Leader   We've arrived, Lord, at your stable. After our long Christmas break, we may feel very much like visitors in a strange land here. So let's listen to the story of some other visitors in the Gospel.

Reader 1   *(Read Matthew 2:1–6)*

Leader   Let us pray.

O God, you revealed your son to the world with a shining star. Guide us today by the light of faith. And lead us to your glory in heaven. Our response is, "Blessed be God forever."

All   Blessed be God forever.

Leader   Now bear with me here, as we finish the Gospel reading.

Reader 2   *(Read Matthew 2:7–12)*

Leader   O God, we too are overjoyed at seeing the star and your son at Christmas. He fills our souls with good things, and we're grateful too. Like the Wise Men, we're bringing you some gifts. We don't have gold, frankincense, or myrrh, but we hope our small gifts are worthy of you today.

All   Blessed be God forever.

Leader   And may we be like the Magi, always choosing the right paths as we continue to spread your love throughout the world.

All   Blessed be God forever.

Leader   Let's begin our new year by saying the prayer our Lord has taught us:

All   Our Father...

In the name of the Father, and of the Son, and of the Holy Spirit. Amen.

"Who's my neighbor?"

WHAT YOU'LL NEED

- **Bible** *(open to Luke 10:29–37)*

THINGS TO DO AHEAD OF TIME

- *Select a volunteer reader.*

- *Copy and print prayer service for your students.*

The Church has designated January as Poverty Awareness Month, but you can use this short prayer service any time, especially with a unit on the parable of the good samaritan.

"Who's my neighbor?"

Gather in your prayer corner and play or sing an appropriate song, such as "God Has Chosen Me" by Bernadette Farrell or "The Cry of the Poor" by John Foley, SJ.

Leader   In the name of the Father, and of the Son, and of the Holy Spirit.

All   Amen.

Reader   *(Read Luke 10:29–37—the parable of the good samaritan)*

Leader   Who's my neighbor? Jesus, help us answer that question.

Right Side   Is my neighbor someone I don't want to talk to?

Left Side   Someone I want to avoid?

Right Side   Is my neighbor someone who is suffering?

Left Side   Someone with a disease I don't want to look at?

Right Side   Someone who is different from me?

Left Side   Is my neighbor a teacher who has it in for me?

Right Side   The kid at school who no one talks to?

Leader   Let's take a few moments to think about this in light of what Jesus says in the Gospel.

(Pause for reflection.)

Leader   And now let's pray for the gift of generosity.

All   Make us worthy, Lord, to serve our neighbor, especially those who live and die in poverty and hunger. Give them, through our hands, their daily bread. And by our understanding and love, give them peace and joy.* We ask this in the name of the Father, and of the Son, and of the Holy Spirit. Amen.

*Based on a prayer by Pope Paul VI.

Jesus in disguise

WHAT YOU'LL NEED

■ **Bible**
(open to Matthew 25:31–46)

■ **Optional**: Find photographs
of homeless or forgotten children,
and create a slide show for use as
you say the prayer

THINGS TO DO
AHEAD OF TIME

■ Select a volunteer reader.

■ Print out a copy of the prayer
service for all.

ere's another prayer you can use during January, or any time you want to show students that Jesus is in everyone they meet. The prayer is based on a quote attributed to Blessed Teresa of Calcutta, who said of the poorest she served, "each one of them is Jesus in disguise."

Jesus in disguise

Gather in your prayer corner and play or sing an appropriate song, such as "God Has Chosen Me" by Bernadette Farrell or "The Cry of the Poor" by John Foley, SJ.

Leader In the name of the Father, and of the Son, and of the Holy Spirit.
All Amen.

Reader *(Read Matthew 25:31–46)*

Leader Let's think about this as we read the poem together.
      The forgotten. The lonely. The diseased.
All Each one of them is Jesus in disguise.

Leader The underprivileged. The underfed. The undernourished.
All Each one of them is Jesus in disguise.

Leader The unwelcome. The unwanted. The unpleasant. The undesirable. The unborn.
All They are Jesus in disguise.

Leader The broken. The fallen. The disgraced. The hurting.
All They are all Jesus in disguise.

Leader The homeless. The hopeless. The defenseless. The faceless. The faithless. (They are all priceless in Jesus' eyes.)
All They are Jesus in disguise.

Leader The despicable. The contemptible. The obnoxious. The nasty. The intolerable.
All They are Jesus in disguise.
      Jesus, we ask for the gift of seeing everyone through your eyes.
      Holy Spirit, we ask for your gift of courage so that we may take action to feed, clothe, care for, and welcome all.
      God our Father, we ask you for the grace of your love, so we may always serve our brothers and sisters in joy, as we serve you.
      In the name of the Father, and of the Son, and of the Holy Spirit. Amen.

Prayer for the sick

WHAT YOU'LL NEED

- **poster board**
- **plastic adhesive-backed bandages**
- **pens** or markers
- **Bible** or lectionary
(open to Luke 5:17–26)

THINGS TO DO AHEAD OF TIME

- *Draw a large heart on the poster board, and cut it out. Display it in or near your prayer corner.*

- *Before the service, ask students to write on the bandages the names of anyone who's sick or in need of healing, and attach the bandages to the poster heart.*

- *Choose readers for the Gospel and petitions.*

While the anointing of the sick is a sacrament instituted by Jesus, and can only be administered by a priest, no doubt you have lots of "absent" marks on your attendance sheet this month, as families battle the flu season. So why not pray together (at least those of you who aren't stuck in bed) for your absentees, and for all who need healing.

We pray for the sick throughout the month of February, beginning with the blessing of throats on February 3, the feast of St. Blase. February 11 is also World Day of the Sick. This observance was instituted by John Paul II and is celebrated every year on the feast of Our Lady of Lourdes.

Prayer for the sick

Leader In the name of the Father, and of the Son, and of the Holy Spirit.
All Amen.

Leader God of mercy, today we pray for all who are sick and suffering, for all who need healing, whether it's physical, mental, or spiritual. And so we listen to the way your son Jesus heals in your name.

Reader *(Read Luke 5:17–26)*

Leader Jesus, at every moment, millions of people all over the world are praying to you. So here we are in the crowd, like the people who brought the man on the stretcher to you. We place the names of our friends here in your presence.

     Let's respond to our prayers of petition with, "Heart of Jesus, hear our prayer."

Reader Lord Jesus, we ask your healing for our friends and family who are sick. Keep them close to your heart. Ease their suffering, if it's your Father's will. Give them comfort and forgive their sins.
All Heart of Jesus, hear our prayer.

Reader Lord, we pray for the families of those who are sick. Strengthen them so they can care for their loved ones without getting discouraged or depressed. Give them courage to get through their toughest days. And when they need it, give them support of friends and helpers.
All Heart of Jesus, hear our prayer.

Reader Jesus, millions of people are sick. People we don't know. We pray for them today. Bless those who are going to have surgery today, and those who will receive painful treatment, like chemotherapy for cancer. Bless especially young kids who are sick and in the hospital. Help them, especially when they're scared and in pain.
All Heart of Jesus, hear our prayer.

Reader   Gentle Jesus, bless all who are in need of healing, whether it's physical, mental, spiritual, or emotional. Let them feel your love and comfort.

All   Heart of Jesus, hear our prayer.

Reader   Lord Jesus, who gives all life, bless the doctors, nurses, and healthcare workers who tend to the sick. Bless their hands, their minds, their hearts, and their work.

All   Heart of Jesus, hear our prayer.

Reader   Finally, Jesus, look at us. Restore anything inside us that needs healing. Breathe your peace into our souls, and cleanse us of our sins.

All   Heart of Jesus, hear our prayer.

Leader   We pray especially to you, Our Lady of Lourdes, on the day that marks the time you showed St. Bernadette the healing waters at Lourdes. You showed the world that your son Jesus truly heals us all. We ask you this in the name of the Father, the Son, and the Holy Spirit.

All   Amen.

Social justice prayer

WORLD DAY OF SOCIAL JUSTICE

WHAT YOU'LL NEED

- **8 poster boards**
- **markers**
- **globe** or world map (optional) to display in your prayer corner

The United Nations' World Day of Social Justice is observed annually on February 20. Of course, it's not a religious feast. And certainly for Catholics, every day is a day of social justice. We see it as prayer in action. This prayer service invites students to pray about ways they can take action on issues of Catholic social teaching.

THINGS TO DO AHEAD OF TIME

- *Write down one general category of Catholic social teaching at the top of each poster:* **Nonviolence, Disarmament, The poor and vulnerable, Rights of workers, Justice, Care for God's creation, Hunger, Sanctity of human life and dignity of the person** *Underneath write "Government,*

Catholic Citizens, Me." Include space between each so that students can write their ideas on what each can do about these issues.

Have a discussion with your class about areas of Catholic social teaching. Have each class member choose one area to commit to. Place the posters around the room, and invite students to stand near the one they've chosen.

Have students brainstorm together about what each group—Government,

Catholic Citizens, Me—can do about these issues. (Explain that Catholic citizens can be adults, while "me" is about what students can do starting right now.) Give students about ten minutes to write their ideas in the categories. Have them choose a spokesperson. When they're finished, invite each spokesperson to explain their group's ideas to the class, and discuss. Then gather by groups around your prayer corner.

73

Social justice prayer service

Leader In the name of the Father, and of the Son, and of the Holy Spirit.

All Amen.

Leader O God, you have a plan for this world. We pray for our government leaders, that they can work together to solve the world's problems. We pray that those who lead our nation and the world are able to...

(Have each spokesperson read the ideas for what governments can do for each issue.)

Leader O God, we are all part of this world you have created. Inspire your people to help with these problems. We pray that Catholic citizens are able to...

(Have each spokesperson read the ideas for what Catholic citizens can do for each issue.)

Leader O God, I may not be able to vote or pass laws, but I can do things that can change the world. I pray for courage to do what's right, starting now. I pray that each of us can...

(Have each spokesperson read the ideas for what each individual ["me"] can do for each issue.)

Leader God, we send you our prayers but we're not stopping here. We want to work for you, for the world, and for everyone. Help us begin by loving others just as Jesus does. Amen.

Good-bye, alleluia

MARDI GRAS

M ardi Gras. Shrove Tuesday. Carnival. Ordinary Time. Lent. Lots of seasons and customs all seem to converge the day before Lent begins. See the Appendix (page 132) for some background on this celebration.

WHAT YOU'LL NEED

■ **sheets of paper** (use high-quality paper if you can find it)

■ **markers**, pastels, or other media

■ **decorated box** (a cardboard box covered in gift wrap or fabric, a cardboard treasure chest [find them at party supply stores], or a wooden box. Some parishes and schools even use small, casket-like boxes)

THINGS TO DO AHEAD OF TIME

■ Make pancakes or buy some doughnuts for a Mardi Gras party. (Make sure you get all your celebrating out of the way before your prayer service.)

■ Decide on a place to "bury" your box of alleluias. It may be a cabinet in the room, or you can simply leave the box at the foot of your prayer corner.

MUSIC SUGGESTIONS FOR PROCESSION

■ **"Alle, Alle, Alleluia"**
by Richard Ho Lung

■ **"Alleluia! Give the Glory"**
by Ken Canedo, Bob Hurd

■ **"Alleluia! Raise the Gospel"**
by Owen Alstott, Bernadette Farrell

THINGS TO DO ON THE DAY OF THE SERVICE

■ Invite your students to write out the word "Alleluia" on the sheets of paper. Let them use their creativity to decorate them. Respect everyone's creativity, but make sure nothing is unworthy or profane. Have them place the alleluias in the box.

■ Choose some volunteers to carry the box toward its resting place.

■ Choose two other volunteers to be prayer leaders.

75

Good-bye, alleluia

Have your students gather in the back of the room, or outside if weather permits. With the Alleluia bearers leading the way, process to your prayer corner, accompanied by a song full of Alleluias. When you arrive at the prayer corner, have the bearers place the Alleluia box at the base of the prayer corner.

Leader In the name of the Father, and of the Son, and of the Holy Spirit.

All Amen.

Prayer Leader 1 Hey, Lord, we've just had one last big celebration before Ash Wednesday and Lent. We want you to be with us, whether we're partying or just being quiet. We want you to be with us during Lent.

Prayer Leader 2 Lord Jesus, we can sing and say "Alleluia" now because we remember how you conquered sin and death. During Lent, though, we remember that we're set apart from our true home with you, because of sin. So we say good-bye to "Alleluia" for a little while.

(Have someone move the box into its hiding place. Turn off any music.)

Prayer Leader 1 Jesus, you told your disciples that you would be betrayed and crucified. They didn't like hearing that. It's pretty hard for us too. But sometimes we have to say good-bye to people, places, and things. It's never easy. So we say, "Good-bye, Alleluia…"

All Good-bye, Alleluia.

Prayer Leader 2 Jesus, you said to your disciples, "If you want to become my followers, deny yourselves and take up your cross and follow me." Sometimes we have to do the same thing. It can be hard putting aside things we're comfortable with. So we say...

All Good-bye, Alleluia.

Prayer Leader 1 Jesus, you didn't enter your real glory until you stretched out your arms on the cross. The world said a sad good-bye to you then. We say it too...

All Good-bye, Alleluia.

Prayer Leader 2 But on Easter we'll celebrate again, as we remember your Resurrection. We'll shout and sing that you have truly risen. Until then, we say it one last time...

All Good-bye, Alleluia.

Prayer Leader 1 In the name of the Father, and of the Son, and of the Holy Spirit. Amen.

And now, we leave our prayer corner, in silence.

(All leave quietly.)

The colors of Lent

ASH WEDNESDAY

Help students remember the three pillars of Lent—fasting, almsgiving, and prayer—with a colorful braided bracelet and a prayer service. It's suitable for the days before or after Ash Wednesday, to help get everyone in a Lenten frame of mind.

WHAT YOU'LL NEED

■ **several colors of yarn**, *cut into 10" lengths (plan for three lengths of yarn per student)*

■ **Bible** *(open to Matthew 6:1–8)*

THINGS TO DO AHEAD OF TIME

■ *Create a sample bracelet by choosing three different colors of yarn. Gather them together and tie a knot at the top. Braid them together and tie another knot at the base. Then bring both ends together and tie. Slip onto your wrist.*

■ *Place lengths of yarn in a basket or other container for students to choose.*

■ *Choose volunteer readers.*

Colors of Lent prayer service

Gather in your prayer corner. Sing or play a recording of an appropriate Lenten song, such as "40 Days" by Matt Maher, or "Beyond the Days" by Ricky Manalo.

Leader In the name of the Father, and of the Son, and of the Holy Spirit.
All Amen.

Reader 1 *(Read Matthew 6:1–8)*

Reader 2 So, Jesus, some things haven't changed much. We still see people who like to show off how religious they are, or how much money they give away. They still don't get it. The real reason we do those things is to get closer to you because, let's face it, we need you, God. We really do. Let's respond, "We need you, God.
All We need you, God.

Reader 3 We need you, God, during these forty days. We don't need the whole world to know we're fasting or praying, but sometimes we need to be reminded about it. So, Lord, we're making something personal to help us remember. By wearing these on our wrists, we're really following your command to "not let your left hand know what your right hand is doing."
All We need you, God.

Reader 4 Guide the work of our hands, Lord, as we make these bracelets. Use our Lenten actions to draw us closer to you.

All We need you, God.

Reader 5 Sure it's hard to give up something we love, Lord. We can't always find time to pray. And we're not always thrilled about sharing with others. We need your help on this.
All We need you, God.

Reader 6 Guide us on these forty days, Lord. Help us wear these bracelets so we will remember the commitment we've made to you today: We follow you, pray to you, love you, and love our neighbor.
All We need you, God.
    In the name of the Father, and of the Son, and of the Holy Spirit. Amen.

Wailing Wall

STUDENT-CREATED PRAYER SERVICE: SESSION 1

Here's something different for Lent. More of a prayer project, this service can cover at least three class sessions, and it's especially timely if you're studying the Old Testament. You'll spend the bulk of the time at your first meeting painting and planning.

WHAT YOU'LL NEED FOR THE WALL

- **butcher paper**
- **thick black marker**
- **tempera paint** (brown and white)
- **pie tins** or flat containers
- **paint brushes** or sponges
- **newspaper**

WHAT YOU'LL NEED FOR THE PRAYER SERVICE

- **Bibles**
- **missals**
- **song collection books**
- **poster boards**
- **scrap paper**
- **pens** and pencils
- **Handouts** 1, 2, and 3

THINGS TO DO AHEAD OF TIME

■ *Make the basis for the wall that students will later paint. Using a black marker, outline the stones of the wall on the butcher paper. You'll want to have at least one stone for each student. You can create the "stones" by drawing a series of horizontal lines, then crisscrossing them with vertical lines. (You may want to work in pencil first.) The lines don't need to be perfectly straight; remember, this is an ancient wall. You can even fill in some corners with black marker to indicate spaces between the stones.*

■ *Make copies of the handouts to help students write the prayer service (see Handout section, page 136).*

OPTIONAL: Search the Internet for photos of John Paul II and Benedict XVI at their visits to the Wailing Wall. You can also find the text of Pope Benedict's prayer at the wall to print out.

THINGS TO DO ON THE DAY OF THE SERVICE

■ *Lay the butcher paper wall on newspaper.*

■ *Add a small amount of brown tempera to the white. You want to achieve a very light brown, almost beige, "stone" color that is light enough for black marker to show through underneath. Place the tempera paint mixture in a few flat pie tins so that everyone can work.*

The Wailing Wall in Jerusalem

A STUDENT-CREATED PRAYER SERVICE: SESSION 1

At the very beginning of class, gather around the butcher paper wall. Explain that today the class will be recreating the Wailing, or Western, Wall of Jerusalem. This is one of the most sacred sites in Judaism. It's the only remaining wall of the second temple in Jerusalem, the one where Jesus taught and prayed. This was the temple where the curtain tore in two at Jesus' death on the cross. Ask if students have seen pictures of the wall, or of people writing prayers on scraps of paper that they put into the cracks between the stones. Explain that today, people of many faiths respect the Wall and its meaning. Pope John Paul II and Pope Benedict have left prayers there. By writing our names here on our own Western Wall, we remember that each of our names is written in God's heart, never to be erased.

Invite each student to choose a brick and write his or her name in it with black marker. (Make sure to write the names of anyone who is absent.) Then allow them to come up, a few at a time, to paint. Have them dip the sponge into the paint and pat it on their brick. Allow the poster to dry throughout class.

While each group paints, others can research the Western Wall, or you can have a discussion about it. After everyone has painted a stone (and you've cleaned up the mess), talk about creating the prayer service.

Discuss the prayer services you've had this year. Ask students what they liked and didn't like. Explain that today, they'll be creating their own prayer service to be said at your Wailing Wall.

Make sure to cover the following:

- *A prayer service can be simple, but each part is important.*
- *At the beginning, we gather and call ourselves into the presence of God. Sometimes there's music.*
- *At some point, a Scripture passage is often read. The service can also have petitions, where we ask others to pray for some special want or need.*
- *At the end of the service, we think about what it all means for us in our lives. This is where we say a closing prayer.*

Divide your class into three groups and give each one of the handouts, along with a poster board and some scrap paper. Encourage everyone to work together and make this prayer service their own.

While the groups are working together, hang up the Wailing Wall in your learning space to dry. When students have finished, gather the groups around it to say their prayer service together. Be careful, as the paint will probably still be wet.

Wailing Wall

STUDENT-CREATED PRAYER SERVICE: SESSION 2

At the second meeting, students add individual prayer intentions.

WHAT YOU'LL NEED

- **Wailing Wall** (see Session One)
- **sticky notes**
- **tape**
- **pens** and pencils
- **Bible** (open to Matthew 7:7–11)

THINGS TO DO ON THE DAY OF THE SERVICE

- *Choose a volunteer reader.*

Wailing Wall

Gather at your Wailing Wall. Sing or play a recording of a song such as "Save Your People" by Jim Farrell or "Turn to Me" by John Foley, SJ.

Leader   In the name of the Father, and of the Son, and of the Holy Spirit.

All   Amen.

Leader   We thank you, Jesus, for bringing us together here at our Wailing Wall, which we now call our Prayer Wall. We come to you humbly as sinners, but with great confidence in your love and mercy.

Now let's pause for a moment and think of all the times we may have offended God this week.

And we'll say an act of contrition together to express how sorry we are for our sins.

All   My God, I am sorry for my sins with all my heart. In choosing to do wrong and failing to do good, I have sinned against you whom I should love above all things. I firmly intend, with your help, to do penance, to sin no more, and to avoid whatever leads me to sin. Our Savior Jesus Christ suffered and died for us. In his name, my God, have mercy. Amen.

Leader   And now let's listen to the word of God.

Reader   *(Read Matthew 7:7–11)*

Leader   Lord Jesus, we're asking, seeking, and knocking. We're also writing.

We place our prayer requests on our wall, just as countless pilgrims have done at the Western Wall in Jerusalem, so close to the temple where you taught, where you were lost for three days, and where you prayed to your Father. We ask you, Lord Jesus, to listen to our prayers.

Give everyone a sticky note and invite them to write a prayer for Lent. Have them fold the notes and place them on the wall. (Use tape to reinforce, if needed.) When all the notes are up, continue with the service.

Leader   O God, let these prayers bring us closer to you. Keep us in your heart always, for we have written our names in the wall of your temple. We offer ourselves to you as a living sacrifice of praise and thanksgiving.

All   Amen.

Leader   In the name of the Father, and of the Son, and of the Holy Spirit.

All   Amen.

Wailing Wall

STUDENT-CREATED PRAYER SERVICE: SESSION 3

WHAT YOU'LL NEED

- **Wailing Wall**
(see Session One)
- **fabric flowers** of all kinds
- **adhesive dots**
- **Bible** (open to John 20:1–9)

THINGS TO DO
ON THE DAY OF
THE SERVICE

- Choose a volunteer reader.

- Display flowers and adhesives near the Prayer Wall so students can decorate.

Time the third meeting for after Easter, when you cover the wall with flowers to symbolize our new life in Jesus' resurrection. You may wish to combine this service with the Easter celebration on pages 103-104.

Wailing Wall

Gather at your class Prayer Wall. Invite students to place adhesive dots all over the wall and attach flowers to them. Try to fill the entire wall with flowers.

Leader   We gather again at our Prayer Wall, Jesus, but today we're here in joy and celebration. Because today we can truly say that you have risen. Alleluia! We've placed flowers here as a symbol of the new life you bring *each of us* through your death and resurrection. Let's shout for joy!

All   Alleluia, Alleluia!

Leader   And now, because it's good to hear the story again and again, we will listen to the Gospel reading about Jesus' resurrection.

Reader   *(Read John 20:1–9)*

Leader   We hear, Lord, and we believe. We thank you for being our paschal sacrifice. Glory to God in the highest.

All   In the name of the Father, and of the Son, and of the Holy Spirit. Amen.

Lenten saint day meditations

A VALENTINE FROM JESUS: LECTIO DIVINA

When Valentine's Day and St. Patrick's Day fall in Lent, it may feel a little strange to create a lot of holiday hoopla. The following meditations can be used during Lent, or any time you want to have a group meditation.

Valentine's Day is a good time to reflect on the real love of God. His agape love for us, which is entwined in charity, is what we hope to spread at this time of year.

WHAT YOU'LL NEED

▨ **Bible**

▨ **candle**

THINGS TO DO AHEAD OF TIME

▨ *Read "Praying Lectio Divina with your Students" in the Appendix (page 130).*

▨ *Choose one of the Scripture passages below, and practice reading it aloud a few times so that you can read it easily in class. You can read them over the course of two class meetings if you want. Just don't read more than one passage at each class meeting.*
1 Corinthians 13:1–13
John 13:31–35

MUSIC SUGGESTIONS

▨ **"Breathe"** *by Marie Barnett*

▨ **"Father, We Adore You"**
by Terrye Coelho Strom

▨ **"Friends for Life"**
by Bob Halligan, Jr.

▨ **"Rain Down"** *by Jaime Cortez*

▨ **"Love Has Come"**
by Matt Maher

A valentine from Jesus

LECTIO DIVINA

Play some instrumental music or one of the selections on page 87. Create some space between each student to minimize distractions. Explain that this is their "me time" with God. Note that while God is always present in our lives, this is our time to really focus on God and to let God focus on us.

Give everyone a few moments to get comfortable. They can lie on the floor if they want.

Leader   This is a good day to have some "me time" with Jesus. Especially this time of year when we give each other valentines and candy and gifts. Today we're going to sit here in Jesus' presence and listen to the valentine he gives us: his love. We'll reflect on the words of the Bible, and think about what Jesus' love means for us. Remember that this is just about you and Jesus. So let's begin.

      In the name of the Father, and of the Son, and of the Holy Spirit. Let's all close our eyes. Take a deep breath, in and out. Let everything go from your day. Put aside the things you are worried about. School. Homework. Chores. Problems. Even friends. This is time for you and God to be alone together. So bring yourself into God's peaceful, loving presence now. Ask the Holy Spirit to be with you and to guide you.

Take a few moments to let everyone be aware of God's presence.

Leader   As I read the following passage from the Bible, listen for any words or phrases that stand out for you.

Read the passage slowly, gently, and calmly. If you are in a church and students are spread out, use a microphone so you don't have to shout.

Leader   Now I am going to read this passage again. Listen for those words or pharses, and this time, think about what God might be saying to you.

Read the passage again, slowly, gently, and calmly.

> **Leader** Now think about what you'd like to say to God. Have a conversation with God, if you want. If you don't know what to say, it's OK; just sit for a while in his loving, peaceful presence. If your mind wanders, don't worry; just bring yourself back to God's presence.

(Pause for a few minutes.)

> **Leader** And now, think about how you might apply any of this to your life, or even to your celebration of Valentine's Day.

(Pause briefly.)

> **Leader** Our meditation is coming to a close, so take a minute to thank God for his presence. And then slowly open your eyes.
>   In the name of the Father, and of the Son, and of the Holy Spirit. Amen.

Play some reflective music as everyone returns to their places.

As always, follow up with a discussion of the process. What worked, what didn't? Make sure everyone understands that there's no right or wrong way to meditate on God's word. If they found themselves getting distracted, help them understand that they can pray to come back into God's presence.

Lenten saint day meditations

HELLO, PATRICK

THINGS TO DO AHEAD OF TIME

■ *Practice the hand movements before the service, so you can demonstrate them easily.*

Although St. Patrick wasn't actually born in Ireland, he adopted the land and its people as his own. We know very little about him, really, but we can imagine his missionary zeal and energy must have been a powerful force for God. With so many secular ways to celebrate this day, why not spend some time with your middle schoolers reflecting on the man and, more importantly, his message.

Hello, Patrick

To get everyone in a reflective mood, play music based on St. Patrick's famous prayer, also known as "The Lorica." Selections might include "Breastplate of St. Patrick" by Sarah Hart, or "Christ Before Me" by Suzanne Toolan, RSM.

Invite everyone to be seated.

Leader   Today, in honor of Saint Patrick, we're going to reflect on the man himself. We're going to imagine ourselves with Patrick on his missionary journeys through Ireland.

So let's begin. Close your eyes and imagine you're on an Irish hillside about fifteen hundred years ago. You've never seen green as rich or as deep as this. There was a mist earlier, but it's lifted now to reveal a sky so blue it makes you feel good just seeing it. You look beyond the hills and you can see the ocean ahead. You think God is wonderful for creating such incredible beauty. And you realize that's why you're here. You're traveling with St. Patrick, telling the people about Jesus. Picture Patrick in your mind: a strong, powerful man who is also kind and sometimes a bit of a joker.

Leader   Imagine Patrick standing in front of you, smiling. He tells you to hold up your hands, palms facing out, away from you and toward him. And yes, I realize he's speaking a foreign language, but you miraculously understand him. Patrick tells you to stretch your thumbs downward to form right angles with your hands. Can you do it? You can open your eyes and take a peek at your hands if you want. *(You may need to repeat the directions here.)* Then Patrick tells you to bring your thumbs together.

(Pause to give everyone a chance to do this.)

Leader Slowly tilt your fingertips toward each other, keeping your thumbs together, so that your index fingers meet. This should form a triangle.

"Look at your hands," Patrick says to you. "There are three sides to the triangle you've formed. Think of each side of the triangle as one person: the Father, the Son, and the Holy Spirit. Each person is distinct, and yet all are one person. That's the Trinity. That's God! Impossible to understand? Yes, but here you are, holding God in your own hands. Think of that!"

St. Patrick takes your hand in his. "Now I realize you're not in Ireland with me," he says. "But I call on you in Jesus' name to spread the Gospel in your world, just as I have. Spread it through your actions, your words, and your love for all." In the name of the Father, and of the Son, and of the Holy Spirit. Amen.

To conclude the prayer service, replay the hymn.

Lenten saint day meditations

AND HELLO, ST. JOSEPH: GUIDED MEDITATION
SOLEMNITY OF ST. JOSEPH, MARCH 19

WHAT YOU'LL NEED

▓ **candle**

THINGS TO DO AHEAD OF TIME

▓ *Read over the suggestions for guided meditation on page 3.*

▓ *Read the meditation before class to familiarize yourself with it.*

Viva la tavola di San Giuseppe! That's the cry often heard on this feast day as St. Joseph Tables overflow with Italian pastas and breads. Other traditions include the famous (some say miraculous) return of the swallows at California's Mission San Juan Capistrano every year on March 19. Whatever way you choose to celebrate this day, consider this guided meditation, to give your students a clearer understanding of the great foster father of Jesus.

And hello, St. Joseph

Gather everyone in your prayer corner, or wherever your class meditates, and light a candle. Begin reading the meditation to your class.

Leader Today we're going to think about St. Joseph, who was Jesus' guardian and foster parent. Let's begin by closing our eyes and putting ourselves in God's presence. Take a deep breath and try to forget about everything else.

(Pause)

Leader Imagine yourself in a place that's very dark. It's so dark your eyes can't get used to the darkness. Then you realize that wherever you are, it smells really bad.

(Pause)

Leader Suddenly you hear a snap. Someone is lighting a piece of flint. There's a little spark of light and in front of you, a bearded man holds up a small torch. You get a look at his face. He looks very kind, but also worried. He holds up the torch to look around. You can slowly see things…straw, and hay, and farm animals. That's where that smell is coming from. There's a cow, and a donkey. Someone is sitting on the donkey, bundled in blankets.

"Are you OK?" the man asks, rushing over.

"Yes, Joseph," a young woman's voice answers, as she unwraps the blankets. "I'm fine. And thank you for finding this place."

As the man, Joseph, helps her down, you see she is pregnant. You're amazed at how gentle the man is with her in this rough place.

"I'm sorry," he says. "It's the best I could do."

"Don't worry," she says gently. "This is what God wants, Joseph. Everything will be all right. Let's pray and thank God for finding this shelter for us."

They join hands. "I will give thanks to the Lord with my whole heart," they say softly. "I will tell of all thy wonderful deeds."

Suddenly the girl stops and puts her hand on her stomach.

And then *(pause)* it's dark again…you feel like you're moving forward in time somehow.

You're not in the stable anymore. You're outside. It's still dark, but the moon is out. You realize you're in the middle of a desert. You look around and there's the man again, Joseph. He's leading the donkey and the young woman is riding it.

She's carrying a small bundle, and you realize it's a baby. Joseph is speaking.

"And so," he says, "I'm sorry, Mary. First Bethlehem, and now Egypt. Once again, I'm dragging you off somewhere. And with a newborn baby."

"But, Joseph," Mary says, "the Lord told you to take us here. You are protecting us from Herod." She holds the baby closer to her.

Joseph shakes his head. "This isn't how I pictured this," he says.

Mary speaks to him very gently. "Joseph, you have always done everything the Lord wants, even when you don't understand why he asks it of you."

Joseph looks up at her. "But Egypt, Mary. It might as well be the moon up there. I've never been to Egypt. I don't even know anyone who's been there. All I know are the stories in the Torah, about my namesake Joseph being sold into slavery in Egypt."

Mary says calmly, "Don't worry, Joseph. The Lord has told you this. This is what he wants for us. I have faith in the Lord. And I have faith in you."

And once again, you suddenly can't see them anymore. But it's getting lighter. You're not in the desert anymore. You're in a room with stone walls. There are wooden chairs and tables everywhere. You smell sawdust and wood. You look around and you see Joseph. He's a little older. A boy is with him, about your age. They wear old clothes like what people wore in Jesus' time. They are building something together. It looks like a table. Joseph is showing the boy how to measure the table. They study the table very carefully, very seriously. Then the boy mumbles something. You don't quite catch it, but whatever it is, it makes Joseph laugh. The two of them laugh so hard they have to stop and sit down.

And now, slowly, that picture is fading too. You don't want to leave, because they look like they're having so much fun, but it's time to come back to our own time. It's time to think and pray about all we've meditated on.

Invite everyone to open their eyes.

Leader And now we'll say a short prayer to conclude our meditation.

St. Joseph, you found a place for Mary when there was no place for her to go.

You kept Mary and Jesus safe. Then when it was time, you brought them home to Nazareth, and you lived a happy, quiet life together until it was time for you to be called home to heaven. We come to you and ask you to protect us too. Pray for us always, St. Joseph, in the name of the Father, and of the Son, and of the Holy Spirit. Amen.

Palm Sunday journey prayer

WHAT YOU'LL NEED

■ **"palm fronds"** *(cut green construction paper into strips to distribute to students. Make enough so that everyone has at least two or three)*

■ **pens** *or markers*

■ **image of Jesus** *for each person (use holy cards or print out an image you like from the Internet. Make copies for each student. [Make sure the image is in the public domain, or that the owner has granted permission to make copies for non-commercial purposes.])*

■ **copies of the Sanctus (Holy) prayer** *(see Handout section, page 138)*

■ **Bible** *(open to Luke 19:28–40)*

Get your class up and moving with this prayer service that reenacts Jesus' triumphal entry into Jerusalem. Students write about their Lenten journeys on "palm fronds" that are strewn in Jesus' pathway.

THINGS TO DO ON THE DAY OF THE SERVICE

■ *Have ready: construction paper "palms," images of Jesus, and Sanctus (Holy) prayer.*

■ *Clear a path in your learning space for a procession.*

Palm Sunday journey prayer

Gather in the back of your learning space. Distribute the palms, and ask everyone to write what they've done on their Lenten journey on them. Examples: Gave up candy, went to confession, donated to a food bank. When you're ready, have them raise their palms high as you make the Sign of the Cross.

Leader In the name of the Father, and of the Son, and of the Holy Spirit. Amen. So it begins. The journey into Jerusalem, and then, Mount Calvary and the cross. For thousands of years, people have retraced Jesus' steps on Palm Sunday with parades and processions. Today, we mark the way too, by remembering our own Lenten journey, and offering it to Jesus.

Allow students to place their palm branches on the path you've cleared to your prayer center. Play a recording of a song such as "We Fall Down" by Chris Tomlin, or "From a King to a King" by Mark Friedman and Janet Vogt. After all the palms have been laid on the floor, the students can return to the back. Distribute the images of Jesus and the Sanctus (Holy) prayer.

Leader Now we walk with Jesus as we listen to the Gospel.

Invite students to walk over the palms, holding the image of Jesus high as you read Luke 19:28–40. When everyone arrives at the prayer center, conclude with the following prayer.

Leader Jesus, our journey doesn't end when Lent is over, or when this class is over. We're journeying our whole lives. It's not always easy, but it's not always difficult either. A lot of it is joyful. Let's sing the song we sing at Mass when we want to praise God.

Sing the Sanctus (Holy) prayer together (see Handout section, page 138).

Leader In the name of the Father, and of the Son, and of the Holy Spirit. Amen.

Have students take the palms and leave them around the prayer center. Let them take the image of Jesus home with them. Invite them to keep it in a place of honor—maybe in their own prayer center.

All you've got

HOLY THURSDAY

WHAT YOU'LL NEED
- Bibles

THINGS TO DO AHEAD OF TIME

- *Print out the prayer service and distribute.*

- *Choose some meditative music to play, such as "Behold the Lamb of God" by Matt Maher.*

We commemorate the Last Supper at every Mass, but the Holy Thursday evening liturgy is special. Church bells ring, and the solemn ritual of footwashing calls each of us to serve others just as our Savior takes care of us. After Communion, the tabernacle is emptied, and the Blessed Sacrament is carried to a temporary resting place.

Most Catholic schools and faith formation programs aren't in session on Holy Thursday, but, using this short service, we can encourage middle schoolers to attend this evening's liturgy with their families. Gather in church if you can. This is a busy day at most churches, so call ahead to make sure yours is open.

All you've got

Bring your Bible to church or another quiet spot. You can speak the prayers aloud together, or read them quietly to yourself.

All   In the name of the Father, and of the Son, and of the Holy Spirit. Amen. Jesus, we're remembering the night before you were condemned to die on the cross. What was it like for you?

(Read the Bible passage quietly to yourself: Mark 14:22–26.)

Right Side   Jesus, you knew what was going to happen to you. And you could have spent this night doing anything. You could have sat at home and let your friends comfort you. But instead of feeling sorry for yourself, you took care of everyone else. After all the miracles, the teaching, the traveling, and all the work, you gave all you had left—your body and blood.

Sit quietly for a few minutes, reflecting on the reading.

Left Side   Jesus, you could have spent this night doing anything. You could have complained. You could have been angry and bitter. You could have run away. Instead, you gave us everything. So how did we repay you?

(Continue reading Mark: 14:32–42.)

Right Side   So your best friends fell asleep on you. After all you gave them, they couldn't even stay awake. It's easy for us to sit here and judge them, Lord, but how many times have we done the same thing? How many times have you needed us, and we've gone our separate ways? Done what we wanted to do?

(Reflect for a few minutes on the reading.)

Left Side   You know where this story is going, Lord. You know it gets worse. You know that we need to read it again.

(Continue reading: Mark 14:43–52.)

All   (*read silently*) And everyone ran away. Again, easy for me to judge. But what would I have done? What do I do today when people betray you, Jesus? I know you love me no matter what. I know you give your body and blood every single day in the Eucharist. So help me stick with you through all my doubts, my fears, and my bad days. On this night, Jesus, you give us all you've got. Let me just think about that for a while.

Reflect quietly for a few minutes on Jesus' incredible love for you in his passion and death. When you're finished, make the Sign of the Cross, and make plans to attend Holy Thursday services with your family.

What's so good about this Friday?

GOOD FRIDAY

WHAT YOU'LL NEED

- **Bibles** *for each student*
- **copies of the meditation** *for each student*

Good question, and it's asked by adolescents (and adults) a lot. The answer is that when Jesus died he showed his infinite, incredible love for us. "No one has greater love than this, to lay down one's life for one's friends."

No Masses are celebrated on this day. We have one job today: to contemplate Calvary, and the deep love that's there. Before sending your students off for Easter break, print out the prayer and give them some time to read it and contemplate.

What's so good about this Friday?

A SILENT MEDITATION AT THE CROSS

Gather before a crucifix. Place yourself in Jesus' presence by making the Sign of the Cross. Take a few deep breaths if you need to, and then read Luke 23:33–43 silently. Afterwards, use the meditation prayer below to help you.

Jesus, as I sit here with you today, I wonder what's so good about today, if something so awful happened. I'm looking at you on the cross, and I'm coming up empty on answers for this one. I can't even imagine all you suffered.

I want to get angry at all these people who have done this to you, Lord. But through the anger, I can hear your voice. "Forgive them." I can hear you giving comfort to the criminal and telling him he'll be with you in Paradise today. This is love I can't even imagine. This is love I hardly know what to do with. This is your love for me, Jesus. This is why this day is so good.

So look down on me, Jesus. I'm kneeling before you. I feel something in my soul, like a burning fire. I pray to you, Lord Jesus, to help me. Keep me just as faithful to you when I walk away from here as I am right now at this moment before your cross. Help me love my neighbor as you do, not just when it's easy, or because that's the answer I'm supposed to give my teachers, but all the time. Help me love even those who persecute me.

I will sit here, Lord, and think about these five wounds of yours: two in your hands, two in your feet, and one in your side. I will remember what your prophet David once said: "They have pierced my hands and my feet; they have numbered all my bones."

I will sit here, Jesus, with you on this good day. And I will love you today and always. Amen.

Remain at the cross for as long as you want. When you're ready, make the Sign of the Cross and go in peace.

Easter celebration

Welcome your students back after the break with a prayer celebration that invites them to enter God's heavenly gates in glory. On this day, encourage boisterousness. Have a procession. Bring in a treat or some baked goods. Let everyone know that it's OK to sing, laugh, and be goofy today. (And yes, it can be cool to sing, even if you're almost in high school.)

If you "buried" the Alleluia, retrieve it joyfully and decorate your learning space with the Alleluias.

WHAT YOU'LL NEED

- **length of white fabric** or bunting
- **copies of "Gloria"** to distribute to students (see Handout section, page 139)
- **"Enter God's gates in glory" poster** (optional)
- **cross** or crucifix
- **paschal candle** (if you have one)
- **symbols of new life** and celebration (Easter lilies, bulb flowers your class has planted, etc.)
- **baked goods** (optional)
- **Bible** (open to Luke 24:1-12)

THINGS TO DO AHEAD OF TIME

- Drape the white fabric or bunting over the doorway to your learning space.

- Display the poster, if you made it.

- Enrich the symbolism by keeping the door locked. Then when you are ready to enter your learning space, have your students open the door with a key—remind them that the key to God's kingdom comes from Jesus.

THINGS TO DO THE DAY OF THE SERVICE

- Place the Bible and the Easter symbols (crucifix, flowers, etc.) on a table outside the doorway.

- At the very beginning of class, meet students outside the door to your learning space. Students will process through the door, symbolizing our entry into God's kingdom.

- Distribute "Gloria" copies as students arrive.

Easter prayer celebration

Leader Today is a day to celebrate. After all those weeks of Lenten preparation—all our prayer, sacrifice, and almsgiving—we are ready to party! Let's hear a loud "Amen!"

All Amen!

Leader Why do we party? Because today we celebrate Jesus' resurrection from the dead into new life. Jesus has won the battle. He's left sin and death behind. So let's honor this victory with our great symbol of life: In the name of the Father, the Son, and the Holy Spirit.

We begin our celebration by proclaiming God's word. A reading from the holy Gospel according to Luke.

Reader *(Read Luke 24:1–12)*
The Gospel of the Lord.

All Praise to you, Lord Jesus Christ.

Leader Yes, praise to you, Lord Jesus Christ, king of endless glory. Today and always we praise you. All creation praises you. You have opened the gates to your Father's kingdom. You invite us all to follow you. And today, we follow!

(Offer the Bible and the symbols to students to carry through the "gates." Make sure they hold these symbols high and with reverence.)

Leader Now we enter your glorious gates as we recite, "Glory to God in the highest."

(Open the door and invite students in as everyone recites the "Gloria" together. Direct everyone to your prayer corner; allow everyone to place symbols there.)

Leader Here we lay our symbols of new life before you, O God.

Saint Paul said, "Christ has become our paschal sacrifice. Let us feast with the unleavened bread of sincerity and truth, alleluia."

All Alleluia!

(If you have prepared baked goods or treats, serve them now. Spend some time in feasting and fellowship with your class. Play some music if you have it. If you have "buried" your Alleluias, now is the time to bring them out and place them at your shrine. Or have a posting party as you and your students decorate your classroom with alleluias.)

Mary crowning

WHAT YOU'LL NEED

- **statue** *or image of Mary*
- **flowers** *of all kinds—students can bring them from home, or they can make them out of tissue paper*
- **containers of water** *for flowers*
- **Mary crown** *(optional)— purchase one from a floral designer, or if you're crafty, make one of your own*
- **rosaries** *for all students (optional)*
- **Bible** *(open to Luke 1:26-38)*

Mary crowning celebrations lost their popularity for a while, but they're back these days, and that's good news for middle schoolers. Not because we enjoy making students sit through long ceremonies in formal attire, but because middle schoolers were always at the heart of Mary crownings. In the old days two eighth graders—a boy and a girl—were traditionally chosen from the parish or school to crown Mary. It was a great honor.

Why not bring back the idea that those who imitate Mary's virtues are to be commended, by choosing two of your students to crown her? Or simply have everyone bring flowers to your statue to show that we are all called to imitate Mary's virtues. There are hundreds of ways to "do" a Mary crowning, and the Blessed Mother is no doubt pleased with even our most humble attempts.

With so many creative ideas on the Internet and in books, we bring you this basic ceremony. Feel free to add or embellish—as long as it does honor to the Mother of God. (Note: a good place to start gathering information about Mary and Mary crownings is the Marian Library/ International Marian Research Institute at the University of Dayton. http://campus.udayton.edu/mary/)

THINGS TO DO AHEAD OF TIME

■ *If you want students to bring in flowers, start sending home reminders and e-mails a few weeks in advance. If you're making the flowers in class, start collecting supplies ahead of time.*

■ *If you're doing the Mary crowning in your prayer corner, make sure you have enough space and plenty of containers for the flowers.*

■ *Consider asking your pastor for permission to crown your parish Marian statue, and make arrangements for a ceremony in church.*

■ *If you're having a big ceremony, be sure to invite parents.*

■ *Talk to students about a dress code. They don't have to buy something new for the ceremony, but certainly they can wear their "Sunday best" to honor our Blessed Mother.*

■ *(Optional) Select, or have students vote on, someone to crown Mary. Remember, it's not a popularity contest. It's about someone who is an example of Mary's faith and selflessness.*

■ *Select volunteer readers.*

Mary crowning prayer service

As students process to the Marian statue, play a contemporary Marian song such as "Be With Us, Mary" by Tom Booth and Jenny Pixler, or a traditional hymn such as "Immaculate Mary." Have them place their flowers in water-filled containers.

Reader   In the name of the Father, and of the Son, and of the Holy Spirit. Amen.

The first words of our prayer are some of the last words of Jesus: "Behold, your Mother."

Today we look at Mary and we see our mother. We honor her as our mother and as queen of heaven and earth.

Please respond, "The Lord has done great things for us; we are filled with gladness and joy."

Reader   Lord God, thank you for your gift of Mary as our model and mother.

She said "yes" to you freely and never ever took it back. We know that her "yes" led her on a difficult path; but Mary knew that you, God, went with her always.

All   The Lord has done great things for us; we are filled with gladness and joy.

Reader   Mary, Mother of Jesus and our beloved Blessed Mother, as we gather around you here today, we believe you are among us, guiding, teaching, and leading us to your son, Jesus.

All   The Lord has done great things for us; we are filled with gladness and joy.

Reader   Teach us by your example how to love Jesus and how to care for one another. Show us what it means to walk with Jesus every day, to stay at the foot of the cross with him, even when everyone else has left.

All   The Lord has done great things for us; we are filled with gladness and joy.

Reader   A reading from the holy Gospel according to Luke. *(Read Luke 1:26–38)*

Sing or play a recording of a Marian hymn while students place a crown on the Mary statue. Then say a decade of the Rosary together, reflecting on one of the Joyful Mysteries.

Spirit party prayer service

PENTECOST

You may not have much energy left by Pentecost to throw a party. But the birthday of the Church is one of the most important feasts of the year. Like the apostles locked away in the upper room, we can hide, but the Spirit will find us to gather in prayer.

So throw a prayer celebration and ask for the Holy Spirit's guidance during the idle days of summer, and ask for help as students prepare for the next school year.

Party in the Spirit

Here are some ideas to celebrate the birthday of the Church and the last days of class:

Drape your prayer corner in the color of the Holy Spirit—bright red (and yellow and orange "flame" colors too).

Throw open the windows and hang strips of red ribbon or crepe paper to flutter in spring's breezes, as a symbol of the Holy Spirit's presence among us.

Bake a birthday cake and decorate it with seven red Lifesaver candies (representing the gifts of the Holy Spirit).

Play some music, such as "Holy Spirit" by Ken Canedo, "Shine, Jesus, Shine" by Graham Kendrick, or "Come Holy Spirit" by Tom Booth.

Pentecost prayer service

Leader In the name of the Father, and of the Son, and of the Holy Spirit. Amen. Today we celebrate the love of our God, poured into our hearts by his Spirit living among us. As we head into summer, and vacations and time away, may we be led by the Holy Spirit.

Reader *(Read Acts 2:1–11)*

Leader Holy Spirit, we adore you and praise you. We thank you for all your graces in our lives. And now we pray for the gifts of the Holy Spirit. Please respond, "Come, Holy Spirit."

All Come, Holy Spirit.

Leader Holy Spirit, give us deep respect for God. Help us steer clear of those who dishonor God in any way.

All Come, Holy Spirit.

Leader Holy Spirit, bring us the gift of piety, so we'll want to be in your loving presence. Help us see the Mass for what it really is: a gift for our souls. Help us find the joy that's waiting for us there.

All Come, Holy Spirit.

Leader Holy Spirit, send your knowledge to us. There's a lot in this world that nobody understands, not even the most brilliant scientists. So help us see that the world's answers aren't always right, and that only you give us true knowledge.

All Come, Holy Spirit.

Leader Holy Spirit, grant us the gift of fortitude. I don't know if you've noticed, but it's tough living in this world. There's temptation everywhere we look. There are people who tell us just to live for today, or do whatever feels right. They try to tell us that anything is OK as long as nobody gets hurt. With your gift of fortitude we can see through the lies to your truth.

All Come, Holy Spirit.

Leader Holy Spirit, give us your gift of counsel. Have we mentioned how tough things are these days? Our decisions aren't easy. So help us by showing us all the sides of every choice. And help us see what God wants for us.

All Come, Holy Spirit.

Leader Holy Spirit, we look for your gift of understanding. Every day, people try to tell us what's important. Maybe it's clothes or games or electronics or money. Maybe it's being popular or famous. Can you keep us grounded, Spirit? Or better yet, can you keep our eyes looking upward, toward heaven? So we can always remember what's really most important?

All Come, Holy Spirit.

Leader Holy Spirit, give us your true wisdom so that we will always stay on the path to God's heavenly kingdom.

All Come, Holy Spirit.

Leader Come, Holy Spirit, fill the hearts of your faithful, and enkindle in them the fire of your love. Send forth your Spirit and they shall be created, and you shall renew the face of the earth.

I give you the words of Blessed Mother Teresa of Calcutta, who was inspired by the Holy Spirit her whole life: "Yesterday is gone. Tomorrow has not yet come. We have only today. Let us begin."

In the name of the Father, and of the Son, and of the Holy Spirit. Amen.

Have a wonderful summer, and God bless you all.

PART 2

Anytime prayers

THESE PRAYER SERVICES AREN'T TIED TO
THE LITURGICAL OR SCHOOL YEAR, BUT THEY'RE
HELPFUL FOR DEVELOPING A DEEP, PERSONAL,
AND LOVING RELATIONSHIP WITH GOD.

Beach ball prayer

WHAT YOU'LL NEED

- **Bible**

(open to Matthew 15:21–28)

- **inflated beach ball**

D on't let the name of this prayer fool you into thinking you can only pray this outside. Try it indoors in a large, empty room such as a church hall. It's especially good during winter when cabin fever hits.

Beach ball prayer

Gather in a circle with plenty of space for everyone to move around. Read Matthew 15:21–28 (the Canaanite woman's faith).

Leader   Jesus sounds like he's being mean here, but he's really making a point. Sometimes when we send our prayers up
(throw the ball in the air and catch it)
it doesn't seem like God answers right away. We have to keep asking
(throw the ball up again and catch it)
and asking
(throw the ball again and catch it)
and asking.
(throw the ball up again and catch it)
It can take a long time. Sometimes
(throw the ball up, but this time, let it fall to the floor)
it feels like God drops the ball on us. Especially when it seems like everything is going wrong.
(pick up the ball)
But we have to pick ourselves up and keep asking. Keep talking. Keep praying. That's what faith is all about. God doesn't always answer our prayers the way we want him to, or when we want him to. But we have to be persistent, like the Canaanite woman. We have to keep our faith strong. And we have to keep talking.

In the name of the Father, and of the Son, and of the Holy Spirit.

Mention something you are praying for. Explain that you'll throw the ball in the air as you send your prayer up. Whoever catches it can do the same. He or she doesn't have to say it out loud, but they should throw the ball in the air. Try to keep the ball up, but if it falls on the ground, point out that we all fall sometimes. The important thing is to pick ourselves up. Continue until everyone has had a chance to toss the ball.

My status update

WHAT YOU'LL NEED

- **pillar candle**
- **Bible** *with the following passages marked:*

2 Timothy 1:1–5

Philippians 1:12–14

1 John 4:16

My status update prayer service

Sit together in a prayer circle.

Leader   Today we're checking in with God for a status update. Nothing formal.

Just letting him know how we feel, where we are, and if there's anything we need. The great thing is that God always "likes" our status. He "loves" it, in fact, just as he loves us always. So let's begin.

In the name of the Father, and of the Son, and of the Holy Spirit. Amen.

God of all love, you want nothing from us except that we love you and love our neighbor. You give us everything we need. Help us experience your love this day. Today we simply want to be in your presence and tell you how we feel.

Let's check some updates from some of Jesus' followers.

Here's one from St. Paul, as he traveled his missionary journeys and wrote to his friend Timothy.
(Read 2 Timothy 1:1–5)

Here's another he posted to a larger group of friends.
(*Read Philippians 1:12–14*)

And here's an update from the Apostle John on his missionary journey.
(*Read 1 John 4:16*)

So let's sit quietly for a minute or two and check in with God. Give him a status update. Let him know what's going on in your life and if you need any help or guidance with anything. Or maybe there's something you want to thank him for. Now is the time to do it.

(Give everyone a few minutes to reflect in silent prayer.)

Leader Lord Jesus, we come to you today in love and hope. We trust in your love for us and your love for the world. Thank you for being with us here.

If anyone would like to add to this prayer, we'll pass around the candle. When it comes to you, feel free to share anything—a prayer, how you feel, whatever. If you don't feel like sharing, that's OK too. Just pass the candle on.

(When the candle returns to you, conclude with the following.)

Leader Thank you, Lord, for hearing us. And now we'll join our prayers together in the way that you taught us.

All Our Father...

In the name of the Father, and of the Son, and of the Holy Spirit. Amen.

Tied up in knots

W hy is it so tough for adults to bring our problems to God? Is it because we didn't get enough practice as young people? Get students thinking about putting their knottiest problems in God's hands with this simple prayer service.

WHAT YOU'LL NEED

■ **String, rope, or cord—** it should be thick enough to provide some visual interest, but thin enough for students to knot easily

■ **image of Jesus** in your prayer center

■ **Bible**
(open to Philippians 4:4-7)

THINGS TO DO AHEAD OF TIME

■ Cut the string into lengths so that students can tie one or more knots in each.

Tied up in knots

This prayer is best done in semi-darkness, so turn down the lights, light a candle, and gather in a prayer circle.

Leader   In the name of the Father, and of the Son, and of the Holy Spirit.

All   Amen.

Leader   Lord, everyone has problems. Some are big, and some are small. Some can tie us up in knots. *(hold up the string as you tie a knot in it)*

Is it true that we can give our problems up to you? What does that mean, exactly? Does it mean we can just leave them with you and then ignore them? Does it mean you'll take our

---

problems away if we pray to you?

Let's listen to what you say about it. *(Read Philippians 4:4–7)*

Lord, you are near, but we are still anxious sometimes. Today we're going to think about our problems for a little while. That's hard to do, so we're going to ask for your help as we face them.

(Distribute the lengths of cord to all present.)

Leader Think of this cord as any problems you might have. Maybe it's a problem your family is facing. *(tie a knot in the cord)* Maybe it's something happening at school. *(tie another knot)* Maybe it involves a friend. *(tie another knot)*

Take your string with you as you go deep into your thoughts. As you think of a problem, tie a knot in the cord. Feel that problem in the cord. Take a look at it. You may have a few problems, so tie as many knots as you need.

Pause for a few minutes to allow everyone to do this. Play a recording of a song such as "Lean on Me" by Bill Withers, or "On Eagle's Wings" by Michael Joncas.

Leader Now, Lord, we come to you. None of us is perfect. Our problems won't go away by themselves. We'll always have something going on. So give us the strength and wisdom to deal with them. Help us remember that when we have problems, that's when you're closest to us. Help us give these problems to you.

Invite everyone to bring the knotted cords to the prayer corner. After they've returned to their seats, continue.

Leader Now, Lord, we've given our problems over to you. They're still ours, but we remember that they're yours too. So we sit in silence here, listening to what you have to say. Maybe we won't hear an answer from you, but we'll keep working on listening to what you have to say.

Pray in silence for a while. When you're finished, make the Sign of the Cross.

Wait. What?

A MEDITATION ON DISTRACTIONS

WHAT YOU'LL NEED

- *Absolutely nothing*

There's a good reason God gave teens such short attention spans. Until we figure that reason out, help them gain something from all those distractions. That is the goal of this group meditation exercise. Try it on a day when everyone is more restless than usual.

Wait. What?

A MEDITATION ON DISTRACTIONS

Gather in your prayer corner or any place where your class can meditate.

Leader How many of you feel like you get distracted easily? What about when you're praying? When you have trouble focusing on your prayers, what can you do?

(Pause for possible answers and ideas.)

Leader These are all good ideas, but today we're going to do something a little different. It might sound strange, especially if people are always telling you to focus and pay attention. Today, I'm asking you to do the opposite. I'm telling you to not pay attention. Go off and think about whatever distracts you. Let your mind wander. Because it's very possible that those distractions are things God wants to talk to you about. Maybe it's a really funny video you can't stop thinking about. Share it with God—he wants to know what makes you laugh. Maybe it's something on T.V. that was really disturbing. Talk to God about it, so he can help you work through it. Maybe it's something you don't think God wants to hear—a mistake you've made, or a sin you've committed. Let your mind go there, but take God with you. Ask his forgiveness and think about not doing it again.

Let's get started by asking God's help.

In the name of the Father, and of the Son, and of the Holy Spirit.

Sometimes, Lord, we get distracted when we pray. We try to get our minds back on our prayers, but it's hard. So today, we're thinking that those distractions might be your way of speaking to us. Help us figure them out.

We'll begin with a prayer together. After we finish, we'll sit in silence for a while and see where our thoughts go. And, God, we're asking you to take us there. Lead our thoughts where you want them to go. If they're bad thoughts, or something that will harm us or others, help us see why they're a problem, and give us the courage to get some help on them. If they're good thoughts, then we hope you enjoy them with us. Oh, yeah. Here I go, getting distracted. So let's begin.

(Begin saying the Our Father and invite everyone to join in. Then spend some time in quiet prayer, letting everyone be alone with their thoughts. Close with the Sign of the Cross. Later, talk about this prayer session and listen to students' feedback.)

Becoming me

Help your middle schoolers discern their abilities and talents, and see where God may be leading them.

WHAT YOU'LL NEED

■ **Bible**
(open to Matthew 25:14–30)
■ **mini flashlights** *or small, flameless candles—one for each person (optional)*

THINGS TO DO AHEAD OF TIME

■ *Choose a volunteer to read the petitions.*

Becoming me

Gather in a prayer circle. If you are using them, distribute the flashlights or candles to all. Turn out any overhead lights, and have everyone turn on their light or candle. Allow everyone to shine them and enjoy the novelty. After a few minutes, begin. You can even let them use the flashlights to bless themselves, if you want.

Leader   In the name of the Father, and of the Son, and of the Holy Spirit. (*Read Matthew 25:14–30*)

All   Amen.

Leader   God in heaven, we are all searching for something. Searching deep down within us for something we can be good at. Some of us have found our talents. Maybe it's a sport. Maybe it's math or music. Maybe it's just being a good listener and a good friend. Some of us, though, have yet to find our talent, our calling. Some of us are still struggling, Lord. We may not feel very good about ourselves.

(If you are using flashlights, direct everyone to turn them off and keep them off until you signal them to go on again. Keep yours on, so you can see.)

Leader So help us, Lord. Help us find our talent—even if it takes a long time. Help us let our light shine for the world. Don't let us bury it, Lord, like the man with the talents in the Gospel. Help us be everything you want us to be.

As we hear these prayer petitions, our response is, "Lord, help us be everything you want us to be."

Reader Jesus, help us accept the hard work that comes with developing our talents.
All Lord, help us be everything you want us to be.

Reader Jesus, help us when we feel we have nothing to offer. Give us patience in seeking our calling.
All Lord, help us be everything you want us to be.

Reader Jesus, keep us prayerful, so that when we need your help, we know you well enough to ask you without being afraid.
All Lord, help us be everything you want us to be.

Reader Help us figure ourselves out, so that we can figure you out.
All Lord, help us be everything you want us to be.

Leader Feel free to add any other intentions.

(Pause to allow students to voice their prayers.)

Leader Pour your divine grace into our hearts, Lord. Transform us with your love. We ask you this in the name of the Father, and of the Son, and of the Holy Spirit.
All Amen.

Have everyone turn on the flashlights again. Sit for a few moments and enjoy the light.

The Beatitudes

CLIMBING TOWARD GOD'S KINGDOM, ONE STEP AT A TIME

WHAT YOU'LL NEED

■ **Bible**
(open to Matthew 5:1–12)

THINGS TO DO AHEAD OF TIME

■ *Print out and copy the prayer service, and select readers to lead each step.*

■ *If you use a staircase, try to schedule this at a time when you won't be interrupted too much, by students changing classes, for instance.*

This prayer service works well with a small group. If your church or school has a staircase that's accessible by your class, gather at the bottom and have students move up one step as you complete each reflection. If climbing stairs is impossible, another option is to sit outside and look up at the sky as you contemplate each of the Beatitudes.

The Beatitudes

CLIMBING TOWARD GOD'S KINGDOM, ONE STEP AT A TIME

Gather at the foot of a staircase or find a spot outdoors, and have everyone read the Bible passage (Matthew 5:1–12) silently. Later, as students read the reflection aloud, invite them to take a step up the stairs together or look up at the sky and contemplate how to put the Beatitudes into action in their lives.

Leader In the name of the Father, and of the Son, and of the Holy Spirit.

All Amen.

Leader Jesus, you've shown us the way to heaven through your words and stories. The problem is that we don't always understand. And you know, Lord, we're not the only ones. Your own apostles had to ask you to explain your parables. So can you help us figure it out? Help us move toward your kingdom one step at a time, by understanding your words. Thanks, Lord.

(After reading each multiple-choice problem, pause for a moment before saying the prayer and moving on.)

Reader 1 Jesus, you say, "Blessed are the poor in spirit, for theirs is the kingdom of heaven." I get closer to your kingdom when I...
      A) think about helping the poor,
      B) think about helping myself to another serving of dessert.

     Jesus, help us take a step toward your kingdom by thinking less about ourselves and more about others.

Reader 2 Jesus, you say, "Blessed are the gentle, for they shall inherit the earth." I get closer to your kingdom when I...
      A) remember that I am the most important person on the planet,
      B) remember that the planet is full of people just like me who are just as important as I am.

Jesus, help us take a step toward your kingdom by helping us remember that there's a world of people out there and that each one has a past, a present, and a future. Give us an interest in others. Give us concern and compassion for all who walk this earth.

Reader 3   Jesus, you say, "Blessed are those who mourn, for they shall be comforted." I get closer to your kingdom when I...
> A) get discouraged and impatient because of all the problems I have,
> B) look away from my problems for a while and focus on the burdens other people are carrying.

Jesus, help us take a step toward your kingdom by helping us remember that when we carry a cross, we join you with yours.

Reader 4   Jesus, you say, "Blessed are those who hunger and thirst for justice, for they shall be filled." I get closer to your kingdom when I...
> A) see an injustice and tell myself it's none of my business,
> B) see an injustice to any human being and decide to help because I am part of the human race.

Jesus, help us take a step toward your kingdom by giving us courage to speak out when we see injustice toward others. Help us to spread your word through our actions.

Reader 5   Jesus, you say, "Blessed are the merciful, for they shall receive mercy." I get closer to your kingdom when I...
> A) see that someone has hurt me and decide they need to suffer for it,
> B) forgive those who hurt me.

Jesus, help us take a step toward your kingdom by helping us forgive quickly, without letting things build up. Keep us from judging others.

Reader 6   Jesus, you say, "Blessed are the clean of heart, for they shall see God." I get closer to your kingdom when I...
> A) remember that I can and should have anything I want because I deserve it,
> B) remember that nothing is free and that everything I take carries a cost.

Jesus, help us take a step toward your kingdom by growing in love for you so that when we're tempted to think only about ourselves, we can look a little farther and see how our decisions affect others. Help us see what impacts our choices might have later in our lives.

Reader 7 Jesus, you say, "Blessed are the peacemakers, for they shall be called children of God." I get closer to your kingdom when I…

  A) am right, and I let everyone know it,

  B) find ways to make peace between people who are arguing.

Jesus, help us take a step toward your kingdom by helping us find opportunities to make peace in our families, our schools, our neighborhoods, our country, and our world.

Reader 8: Jesus, you say, "Blessed are those who are persecuted for the sake of justice, for the kingdom of heaven is theirs." I get closer to your kingdom when I…

  A) agree with everyone else about something I know is wrong, because the cost of speaking out is too high,

  B) realize that speaking up for something that's right may cost me friends and popularity, and I speak up anyway.

Jesus, help us take a step toward your kingdom. There may come a time when we have to suffer for what is right, rather than practice injustice. Build up our strength and courage. Make us willing to suffer for the sake of right instead of practicing any injustice; keep us from discriminating against anyone we perceive as different.

Leader Jesus, we're here. Your fantastic, amazing kingdom is right here on earth. And we're part of it every time we do what's right and good. Thank you for bringing us here. Keep us moving forward, moving upward, toward your eternal kingdom in heaven. In the name of the Father, and of the Son, and of the Holy Spirit.

All Amen.

Be not afraid

PRAYER IN NATIONAL EMERGENCY, DISASTER, OR STRESS

WHAT YOU'LL NEED

- **candle**
- **copies of the Memorare of St. Bernard** (see Handout section, page 139)
- **one of the following readings** (choose depending on the circumstance)
  Matthew 10:26-31
  John 14:1-6, 27
  Mark 4:35-41
  Matthew 14:22-33
  Matthew 28:1-10

MUSIC SUGGESTION

"Be Not Afraid" *by Bob Dufford*

Many middle schoolers are far more aware of what's going on in the world than we realize. Use this prayer in times of a national emergency, a major disaster, or any kind of stress.

Prayer in national emergency, disaster, or stress

Offer a spontaneous prayer or use the following:

Leader In the name of the Father, and of the Son, and of the Holy Spirit.

All Amen.

Leader Lord, so much is happening in our world right now. We hear people wanting to blame you. Others want to blame the world for being so sinful or stupid. But they're not really helping the situation, Lord.
What we really need is to listen to what you always say: "Be not afraid."
Be not afraid.
We put our faith, hope, and trust in you alone, Lord.
Be not afraid.
To help us out, we're going to listen to your words right now.

(Choose any of the readings on page 126 to read.)

Leader Jesus, we know you're with us, even if we can't see you. We also know you give us extra help in difficult times. You ask your mother, Mary, to comfort us. So we turn to both of you now, as we pray.

(Pray the Memorare together [see Handout section, page 139].)

Leader Now please join me in these simple words that can bring great confidence. We'll repeat them three times. As you say the words, feel Jesus' love and strength fill your heart.

All Jesus, I trust in you.
Jesus, I trust in you.
Jesus, I trust in you.

Leader In the name of the Father, and of the Son, and of the Holy Spirit.

All Amen.

Coming together

PETITION SERVICE

WHAT YOU'LL NEED

- **pitcher of water**
- **clear plastic bowl**
- **Bible**

(open to Matthew 18:19–20)

Use this general petition service on a regular basis so students can get comfortable voicing their prayer needs. It can also help them develop a habit of praying for others.

Coming together

GENERAL PETITION SERVICE

Gather together in a prayer circle with the pitcher of water and bowl in the center.

Leader   In the name of the Father, and of the Son, and of the Holy Spirit.

All   Amen.

Leader   Lord Jesus, you said: "If two of you agree on earth about anything for which they are to pray, it shall be granted to them by my heavenly Father. For where two or three are gathered together in my name, there am I in the midst of them" (Matthew 18:19–20).

So, Lord Jesus, here we are, gathered in your name. Thanks for being here with us.

Invite students to come forward one at a time, and pour a little of the water into the bowl. Explain that by doing this, we show that each person's prayer is everyone's prayer. Students who don't want to share out loud can simply say, "Please pray for a special intention," and pour the water in the bowl. Choose a response, such as "Lord, hear us." When all of the water has been poured into the bowl, conclude with the following.

Leader   Lord Jesus, thanks for hearing our prayers today. We know that one prayer can become many when we gather in your name. So let's pray together.

All   Our Father, who art in heaven...
In the name of the Father, and of the Son, and of the Holy Spirit. Amen.

APPENDIX 1: ESSENTIALS

Planning a prayer center with your class

Spend some time thinking about your classroom and how you can incorporate a prayer center into it. Do you meet in a parish hall or a classroom that other students use during the day? If so, you'll probably need to pack up your prayer corner at the end of every class.

Find a location with enough room for all your students to gather comfortably. Or, if that's impossible, make it a visual focal point, so that everyone can easily see it no matter where they sit.

Give your prayer corner a basic structure or support, such as a table or desk. If your prayer center is a permanent fixture, consider adding a chair for individual meditation. If your students will create the prayer center entirely, start them off with one element, such as a crucifix or a Bible, to identify the space.

Although you want to give students some creative freedom, it's fine (and probably necessary) to offer some guidance, ideas, and structure. Here are a few different directions to take:

Items from home. Create a basic prayer center yourself, and then plan a week where everyone brings items from home to add to it. Or assign one individual each week. Be sure to ask if it's okay to keep the elements in the school prayer corner for a while, or if students would like to bring them home the same day. (See the reproducible Parent Permission/Reminder in the Handouts section, page 133).

Artwork. Develop the basic prayer center, and have your class create an element together. Here are some ideas:

- Tissue paper flower decorations. (You can change the colors to correspond to the liturgical seasons.)
- Hand-painted prayer cloth. Students paint their names or handprints on a piece of fabric that is draped over the prayer table.
- Bible quotes backdrop. Students look through their Bibles to find quotes that really speak to them. They copy the quotes on colorful paper, which you tape to a poster board.

Praying lectio divina with your students

The practice of lectio divina (divine reading) is an old one. The idea is to read a Scripture passage several times, slowly and carefully. You pick out a word or phrase that speaks to you, and you then reflect on the meaning God has in mind for you.

Once you help middle schoolers understand how to meditate, you'll find that they actually enjoy the process. And so will you. Here are a few tips:

Give everyone lots of space. Decide ahead of time on a place to gather. Your church is best, but any place that offers a prayerful atmosphere free of distractions is fine— for example, your prayer corner, another classroom, or a multipurpose room. Unless you have a regular gathering space there, avoid going outside, as it can be terribly distracting.

Make sure there's enough room to seat your entire class without crowding everyone. The last thing you want are tight little bunches of students gathered together. As everyone gathers, create some space between each student to minimize distractions. If you're in church, seat just one person to each pew. Explain that this is "me time" with God. While God is always present in our lives, this is a time to really focus on God and let God focus on us.

Focus on reading. Before you read the passage to your students, practice reading it aloud. Be a relaxing, prayerful presence for your students, so they can follow your lead. If you meet in a church and students are spread out, use a microphone so you don't have to shout. If you're worried about something, or feeling stressed or distracted, consider having someone else take over for you.

The process

1. Take a few moments to let everyone be aware of God's presence. Explain that you are going to read a Bible passage

to them. Ask students to listen for any words or phrases that stand out for them.

2. Read the passage slowly, gently, and calmly. Give everyone time to reflect on it.

3. Read it again, telling everyone to listen again for those words or phrases and, this time, think about what God might be saying to them.

4. Invite students to think about what they'd like to say to God. Invite them to have a conversation with God, if they want. If they don't know what to say, tell them it's okay, they can just sit for a while in his loving, peaceful presence. If their minds wander, tell them to bring themselves back to God's presence.

5. Finally, ask them to think about what they might want to change in their lives as a result of the Scripture. Tell them to ask for God's help on this.

6. Give them some time to meditate, and have them thank God for his presence. Ask them to open their eyes.

Follow up with a discussion of the process if you'd like. What worked, what didn't? Make sure everyone understands that there's no right or wrong way to mediate on God's word. If they find themselves getting distracted, help them understand that they can pray to come back into God's presence.

Create a class shrine to honor the dead

No matter how you honor the dead, plan to keep your shrine up throughout the month of November. Use photos, memorabilia, and symbols from nature such as autumn leaves or dried flowers. A cross or crucifix should be the centerpiece, as a symbol of the life that is stronger than death. Everything should be full of beauty and honor. Here are a few ideas:

- Ask students to bring in photos or mementoes of loved ones who have died. During the prayer service, they can bring them to the shrine. (Be sure to bring in your own photos, and consider asking other members of the staff, including your parish priests, to offer photos as well.)

- If photos are impossible, ask students to write the names of departed loved ones on slips of paper. During the service, they can place the names in a cloth-lined basket. Or have them write the names in a beautiful blank book. Give the basket or book a place of honor in your shrine.

- If a beloved member of your community has died recently, include his or her photo in your shrine too.

- Refer to your parish bulletin and have students copy the names of those who have recently died onto poster board or into a blank book. Make sure students use their best handwriting to honor these faithful departed.

A bit of background about Mardi Gras

Mardi Gras means Fat Tuesday. It's an old French term referring, probably, to the fatted calf that was eaten before the fast of Lent. Its English equivalent is Shrove Tuesday. (Shrove means "to confess.") The idea was that you confessed your sins the day before Ash Wednesday so you knew what sort of penance you'd be dealing with during Lent. It was sometimes known in England as Pancake Tuesday because of the old tradition of eating pancakes, most likely as a means to use up the last of the eggs, sugar, and lard before the fast. In Poland, revelers feasted on fried doughnuts called pączki, probably with the same idea in mind.

The season of Carnival, or Ordinary Time on the liturgical calendar, spans the time from the Epiphany in January to Mardi Gras. (Carne vale means a farewell to meat).

Why not show students how all the feasts are connected? We end the period of Ordinary Time and begin the season of Lent on Ash Wednesday, when we say good-bye to creature comforts and the merrymaking of Carnival. A sign of the somberness of Lent is the absence of the Alleluia at Mass. So it's a good time to say good-bye, with the centuries-old tradition of burying the alleluia. Have one last feast before the fast if you can. Maybe you can serve up some pancakes and doughnuts today too.

APPENDIX 2: HANDOUTS

① PARENT PERMISSION/REMINDER

I'm helping to build something for God. I'm bringing something to contribute to the prayer corner in our classroom.

I'm bringing it on (date): _____

Item: _____

I will bring the item home on: _____

Parent Signature: _____

Parents,

Your child is invited to bring something from home to our class prayer corner. It can be something meaningful to your child or your family that he or she is willing to share in the prayer corner. (Please do not buy something new—this is about sharing what we have with God.)

Please keep this note in a safe place and remind your child to bring in the item on the date indicated. You may want to label the item with your family name. Examples of items to bring are:

☐ rosary ☐ crucifix or cross ☐ saint statue
☐ family Bible ☐ holy water font ☐ holy cards
☐ blessed candles
☐ family photos from baptism, First Eucharist, or a picture of a relative who has passed away
☐ items from nature that represent God's creation and presence (a pine cone or seashell from a vacation, a rock from the back yard, dried leaves, flowers, etc.)

Thank you for your help in creating something beautiful for God and your child!

② PRAYER OF ST. TERESA OF AVILA

Christ has no body now but yours
No hands, no feet on earth but yours
Yours are the eyes through which he looks with compassion on this earth
Yours are the feet with which he walks to do good
Yours are the hands with which he blesses all the world
Yours are the hands
Yours are the feet
Yours are the eyes
You are his body
Christ has no body now on earth but yours.

- -

③ SAINTS WHO FASCINATE US

All of the saints here have fascinating stories. Use this list with the Litany of Saints on page 33. Print out the sheet and cut out the individual names. Place the names in a basket for students to choose from. Feel free to add more if you want.

Angela Merici
Josephine Bakhita
Saint Teresa Benedicta of the Cross
    (Edith Stein)
Catherine of Siena
Teresa of Avila
Joseph Cupertino
Francis of Assisi
Miguel Pro
Martin de Porres
Anthony of Padua
Francis Xavier
Maximilian Kolbe
Pio of Pietrelcina (Padre Pio)
Ignatius of Loyola
John of the Cross
Joan of Arc
Bernadette

Maria Goretti
Paul of the Cross
Damien of Molokai
Stanislaus Kostka
Sebastian
Aloysius Gonzaga
Agnes, Agatha, and Lucy
Catherine Labouré
Kateri Tekakwitha
Charles Lwanga
Paul Miki and companions
Clare
Margaret Mary Alacoque
Margaret of Cortona
Rita
Philip Neri
John Bosco
Mary, Queen of the Saints

④ THE CONFITEOR PRAYER

I confess to almighty God
and to you, my brothers and sisters,
that I have greatly sinned
in my thoughts and in my words,
in what I have done
and in what I have failed to do,
through my fault, through my fault,
through my most grievous fault;
therefore I ask blessed Mary ever-Virgin,
all the Angels and Saints,
and you, my brothers and sisters,
to pray for me to the Lord our God.

---

⑤ THE HAIL MARY IN SPANISH

Dios te salve, Maria.
Llena eres de gracia:
El Señor es contigo.
Bendita tú eres entre todas las mujeres.
Y bendito es el fruto de tu vientre:
Jesús.

Hail Mary,
full of grace
the Lord is with you.
Blessed are you among women
and blessed is the fruit of your womb,
Jesus.

Santa María, Madre de Dios,
ruega por nosotros pecadores,
ahora y en la hora de nuestra muerte.
Amén.

Holy Mary, mother of God,
pray for us sinners
Now and at the hour of our death.
Amen.

⑥ HANDOUTS FOR "WAILING WALL" PRAYER SERVICE

GROUP 1 HANDOUT: Gathering music and opening prayer

You've been asked to come up with some opening music and an opening prayer for your class prayer service. Jot down your ideas on scratch paper and when everyone agrees on what to do, have someone write the "script" for your section on poster board. Remember, you're in charge of this section. Whatever your group decides to do, everyone in your class will be a part of it.

- A prayer service can use any of the following:
    silence (some time to reflect)
    movement (such as raising our hands to praise God, a procession where we sing or pray as we move toward God, or touching a symbol such as a crucifix to show reverence)
    visual elements (such as a candle)
    sacramentals (like holy water)

- Start by choosing some music for your opening song. For ideas, your parish hymnal can get you started.

- Once you've agreed on a song, write the opening prayer. Remember to begin the service as you would any prayer, with the Sign of the Cross. Some prayer starters include:
    Let us pray...
    We come together today, Father...
    We ask your blessing, Jesus...
    Jesus, we are beginning the season of Lent. Help us...

- Remember to choose someone to read the prayer service. Someone else may need to hold the poster board.

HANDOUTS FOR "WAILING WALL" PRAYER SERVICE

GROUP 2 HANDOUT: Scripture and reflection

You've been asked to choose a Scripture reading and offer some thoughts about it for your class prayer service. Jot down your ideas on scratch paper and when everyone agrees on what to do, have someone write the "script" for your section on poster board. Remember, you're in charge of this section. Whatever your group decides to do, everyone in your class will be a part of it.

- Start by choosing the Scripture reading. Some passages related to Lent include:
  Genesis 7:17–20   *Genesis 8:6–12*
  Exodus 3:1–8, 13–15   *Joel 2 12–18*
  Matthew 6:1–6   *Luke 4 1–13*

- Remember to begin the Scripture reading with: *"A reading from…"*

- At the end of the reading, say something like *"The word of the Lord."*

- Next, think of some ideas for the reflection. It can be anything you want to say about the reading. Your reflection can use any of the following:
  silence (some time to reflect)
  movement (such as raising our hands to praise God or touching a symbol such as a crucifix to show reverence)
  visual elements (such as a candle)
  sacramentals (like holy water)

- Remember to choose someone to read the Scripture passage aloud. Someone else may need to read from the poster board.

HANDOUTS FOR "WAILING WALL" PRAYER SERVICE

GROUP 3 HANDOUT: Petitions and closing prayer

You've been asked to write the petitions and closing prayer for your class prayer service. Petitions are people or situations we want to ask everyone to pray for. They can be general, like "for the world, that all nations may be at peace," or specific, like "for the Holy Father, that he may lead us toward Jesus this Easter, " or "for my aunt, who's sick." Jot down your ideas on scrap paper and when everyone agrees on what to do, have someone write the "script" for your section on poster board. Remember, you're in charge of this section. Whatever your group decides to do, everyone in your class will be a part of it.

- Start with the petitions. Everyone should be able to come up with at least one.

- Then agree on a way to ask for prayers, like *"We pray to the Lord...."*

- Come up with one response you want people to say, like *"Lord, hear our prayer."*

- Then you can write the closing prayer. You can say a standard prayer, or write your own prayer together. Write your prayer on the poster board. Then write your prayer script for the closing. Something like this:

   Thank you, Father, for hearing us today. As we go forth, we praise you every day in every way. May the almighty and merciful Lord, Father, Son, and Holy Spirit, bless and keep us.

- Be sure to end with an *"Amen"* and the Sign of the Cross.

- Remember to choose someone to read the prayer service. Someone else may need to hold the poster board.

---

⑦ SANCTUS (HOLY)

Holy, Holy, Holy Lord God of hosts.
Heaven and earth are full of your glory.
Hosanna in the highest.
Blessed is he who comes in the name of the Lord.
Hosanna in the highest.

⑧ GLORIA

Glory to God in the highest,
and on earth peace to people of good will.
We praise you, we bless you, we adore you,
we glorify you, we give you thanks
for your great glory, Lord God,
heavenly King, O God, almighty Father.
Lord Jesus Christ, Only Begotten Son,
Lord God, Lamb of God, Son of the Father,
you take away the sins of the world,
have mercy on us;
you take away the sins of the world,
receive our prayer;
you are seated at the right hand of the Father,
have mercy on us.
For you alone are the Holy One, you alone are the Lord,
you alone are the Most High, Jesus Christ,
with the Holy Spirit,
in the glory of God the Father. Amen.

---

⑨ ST. BERNARD'S MEMORARE

Remember, O most gracious Virgin Mary,
that never was it known that anyone
who fled to your protection,
implored your help,
or sought your intercession
was left unaided.
Inspired with this confidence,
I fly unto you,
O Virgin of virgins, my Mother!
To you I come, before you I stand,
sinful and sorrowful.
O Mother of the Word Incarnate,
despise not my petitions, but in your mercy,
hear and answer me. Amen.

ALSO BY **CONNIE CLARK**

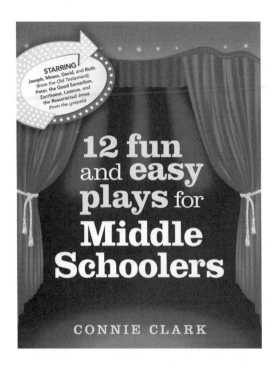

12 Fun and Easy Plays for Middle Schoolers

Share the Bible and saint stories with middle schoolers by letting them "stand up, stretch out, talk, whisper, and even shout." This unique resource makes drama a part of curriculum and is packed with lesson plans that include reproducible scripts, prop lists, prayers, discussion questions, and more.

184 PAGES • $19.95 • 978-1-58595-764-4
ORDER 957644

OUR PARISH AT PRAYER

A Prayerbook for Confirmation Candidates

These beautiful prayers capture the emotions and attitudes of teenagers preparing to be confirmed. They express the doubts and fears of adolescents and ultimately the joy of conversion to Christ through the Holy Spirit. A perfect daily companion for all confirmands. Bulk pricing* is available.

*Bulk pricing for OUR PARISH AT PRAYER	
1-49 copies	99¢ each
50-99 copies	79¢ each
100-499 copies	59¢ each
500+ copies	49¢ each

32 PAGES • 99¢ • 978-1-58595-811-5 • ORDER 958115

TWENTY THIRD *23rd*
PUBLICATIONS

1-800-321-0411
www.23rdpublications.com